DEATH *in* North Carolina's Piedmont

DEATH
in
North Carolina's Piedmont

Tales of Murder, Suicide and Causes Unknown

Frances H. Casstevens

The History Press

Published by The History Press
Charleston, SC 29403
www.historypress.net

Cover image courtesy of Roger Kammerer.

First published 2006

Manufactured in the United States

ISBN 978.1.59629.196.6

Library of Congress Cataloging-in-Publication Data

Casstevens, Frances Harding.
Death in North Carolina's Piedmont : tales of murder, suicide and causes unknown / Frances H. Casstevens.
p. cm.
Includes bibliographical references.
ISBN-13: 978-1-59629-196-6 (alk. paper)
1. Murder--North Carolina--Case studies. 2. Suicide--North Carolina--Case studies. I. Title.

HV6533.N8C37 2006
364.152'3097565--dc22
2006025847

Contents

ACKNOWLEDGEMENTS

I wish to thank the staffs of the Yadkin County Public Library, the Forsyth County Public Library, the North Carolina Division of Archives and History and the Library of Congress for their assistance.

Thanks to my good friend Kim Quintal. She has inspired me and given me the confidence to continue writing. My appreciation goes to Michael Renegar for his suggestions and information about forgotten crimes.

Charles White furnished census records on some of the individuals that helped round out a fuller picture of them and their families.

I appreciate the information Faye Moran shared via her web page. My thanks also go to Attorney Greg Luck for information concerning the trials of Tom Dula.

Esther Johnson shared information regarding the Lawson family murders and Linda Allman took a photo of their graves.

Thanks to Greg Cheek, Andrew Mackie and the Yadkin County Historical Society for pictures they have permitted me to use.

Lastly, I want to thank the staff of the Yadkin County Register of Deeds office, especially Aric Wilhelm, for their constant care of county records, without which much of our history would be lost.

Introduction

We are a people fascinated by gruesome crimes, horrible murders and mysterious disappearances. If the crime is unsolved, our interest is even greater. In the case of a suicide, if the reason for it is unknown, it intrigues us.

This morbid curiosity is reflected by the increasing number of television series and motion pictures centered on crime. With the advent of new pathological and forensic techniques, medical technicians can often solve crimes that have baffled law enforcement officers. With advances in DNA testing, more and more criminals are convicted and on occasion the wrongly convicted are freed.

This work is an odd assortment of untimely deaths. Some were crimes that happened so long ago it is doubtful any new information will ever be discovered to alter the verdict or place the guilt on another person. The perpetrator of a crime can remain unknown for so long that the case is finally dropped. However, murder is a capital crime and the criminal, if found, can still be prosecuted many years after the crime was committed. There is no statute of limitations for the crime of murder.

Whether the death of a person was the result of murder or suicide is often very difficult to determine. If a person has disappeared, it is uncertain whether a crime has been committed or whether the person chose to disappear. Even if a crime is suspected, it is difficult to convict a suspect without finding the body of the victim of the crime.

Some crimes forever remain in that gray area where the truth seems apparent one moment, but in the next moment doubts creep in. Some of these cases tend to remain in the deep recesses of our minds, and occasionally we think of them and wonder what really happened. It may be that we don't want to know the truth nearly as much as we enjoy the mystery.

Who Killed Captain James West?

Thee will get thy head shot off thy shoulders.

A light snow was falling and the weather had turned bitterly cold. Jesse Dobbins, his brother William and about a dozen men had taken shelter in the Bond School before starting out across the mountains. All of them were evading the Confederate conscription laws. One or two of the men were deserters from the Confederate army. William Dobbins had recently escaped from the Yadkin County jail, where he was being held for "draft dodging."

In addition to those who did not believe in Secession and those evading the draft, there were many Quakers in the county who did not believe in either war or slavery. Most of the population of Yadkin County were farmers of small tracts of land. Only a few owned enough acreage that a large number of slaves was needed to do the work on the plantation.

The school was on a knoll on the south side of the branch that meandered behind Deep Creek Friends Church. The men thought they were safe inside the school, but someone saw them entering the little log school building. That unknown person went on to Yadkinville and reported what he had seen to the authorities. Shortly afterward, James West gathered a group of local militia to apprehend the fugitives. The militia was reported to number between twelve and fifty-six local men. No one knows for sure just how many there were.

On the way to the school, West and his men passed the home of Daniel Vestal. They stopped to get a drink of water from the well in the front yard of the Vestal place. West divulged his destination and told Mr. and Mrs. Vestal that he was going to the Bond School to arrest the men hiding out there. Mrs. Vestal, a devout Quaker, replied, "Yes, and thee will get thy head shot off thy shoulders, too." Her words proved prophetic.

Inside the little school, the men were relaxing around the fireplace. Several were reading the latest war news in a newspaper and another man was eating a sweet potato. Jesse Dobbins had avoided conscription so far because he had

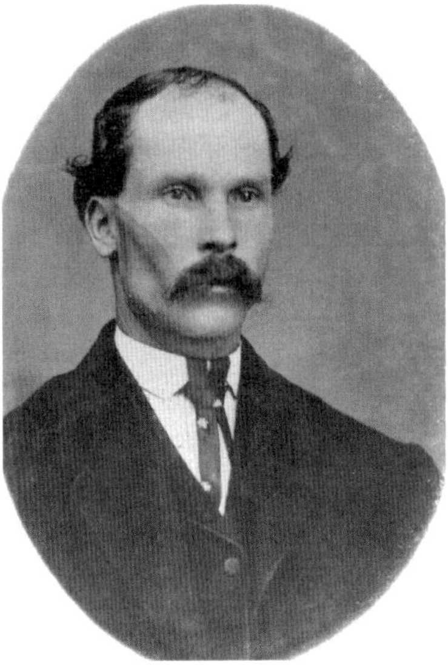

Captain James West, militia leader killed in the Bond School shootout. *Collection of Frances H. Casstevens.*

been employed to haul salt from Saltville, Virginia, back to Yadkin County. Only recently had his exempt status changed. His brother William had been arrested before February 12 and taken to jail. He had escaped and had been hiding in the woods until he joined the group in the school.

The men in the school were not all Quakers, although some joined that church later. Several of the men were brothers: Jesse and William Dobbins; Benjamin, Lee and William Willard; John, Anderson and Sanford Douglas; Horace and Eck Allgood. Others were not brothers but some of them were probably related: Thomas Adams, Enoch Brown, James Wooten, Robert Hutchens, Hugh Sprinkle and Solomon Hinshaw.

Suddenly, they heard someone at the door and a voice said sternly, "Open up in there. You are all under arrest." The group in the schoolhouse that morning was unprepared for the arrival of the militia but they quickly grabbed their muskets and guns to defend themselves.

The door was jerked open to reveal Captain James West standing on the large stone doorstep. A moment later, West fell backwards, dead with a bullet in his head. Pandemonium reigned. Shots were fired from the militia into the schoolhouse and the men inside returned their fire. When it was all over, four men lay dead, two on each side—Captain James West and John Williams of the militia and Sol Hinshaw and Eck Allgood from inside the school.

Several of the militia were wounded. Some of the conscripts fled out a window on the back of the school and without Captain West to give the order for pursuit, the men escaped capture.

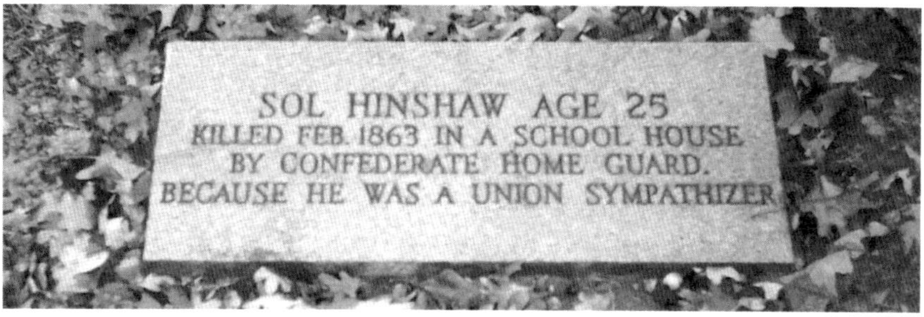

Tombstone of Sol Hinshaw, conscript killed in shootout at the Bond School, Deep Creek Friends Church cemetery. *Photography by Frances H. Casstevens.*

According to Ms. Ruby F. Hinshaw, Sol Hinshaw was the first man killed inside the schoolhouse. She believed the militia had come to kill Jesse Dobbins because he had threatened the militia. She was told that Dobbins slid down under a bench to avoid being shot, then escaped out the window. Local tradition states that the Willard boys did most of the shooting. Murphy Gabard, one member of the militia, recalled that he stood behind a tree and saw one of the Willard boys shoot Captain West.

Indictments were drawn up against fourteen of the sixteen in the school for the murder of James West and John Williams. The indictment centered on Jesse Dobbins, indicted as the person who—with a certain rifle made of iron and steel of the value of one dollar charged and loaded with powder and one leaden bullet of no value—shot James West on the left side of his head close to his left eye. The bullet penetrated to a depth of six inches and West died instantly.

After the encounter, Attorney R.F. Armfield wrote Governor Zebulon B. Vance for advice:

> *Militia officers came on 16 of these desperadoes in a school house about 4 miles from this town, armed, fortified, and ready for the fight. The firing immediately commenced, which side fired first is not positively certain, but from the best information I can get I believe it was those in the school-house. They finally fled, leaving 2 of their number dead and carrying off 2 wounded, after killing 2 of the officers. In the school house were found cartridges of the most deadly and murderous quality, made of home-made powder (one of the men known to have been among them has been engaged in making powder). Four of the conscripts who were in the fight have since come in and surrendered and are now in jail here, but the leaders and the most guilty of them are still at large; and the section of the country in which they lurk is so disloyal (I grieve to say*

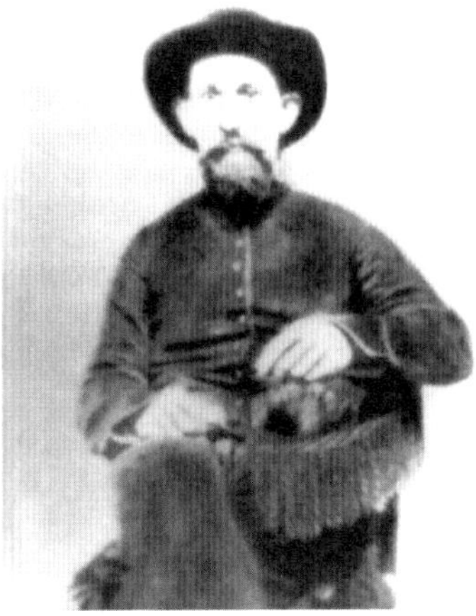

Jesse Dobbins was accused of Captain West's murder. *Courtesy of the Yadkin County Historical Society.*

> *it), and the people so readily conceal the murderers and convey intelligence to them that it will be exceedingly difficult to find them.*

DOBBINS RETURNS HOME

Jesse Dobbins escaped without injury and he and several others fled the county to join the Union army. The little group traveled across the Blue Ridge Mountains, through Tennessee and into Kentucky—almost five hundred miles in very cold weather. Jesse enlisted in the Fourth Ohio Battery, then transferred to the First Tennessee Battery.

Their journey took less than twelve days. According to his service record, Jesse Dobbins enlisted on February 27, 1863, at Lexington, Kentucky, for a period of three years. He was described as thirty-four years old with dark hair and eyes and was about five feet ten inches tall.

Jesse attributed the death of his brother William Dobbins to their flight in the dead of winter. The weather was so cold his clothes often froze to his body. However, William did not die until the fall of 1864, a year and a half after the brother fled Yadkin County. The hardships he endured could, however, have been a contributing factor in his demise.

When the war ended, Jesse Dobbins returned to his wife and family in Yadkin County. Even though the war was over and the South defeated, there was resentment against Jesse Dobbins because of the shootout at the school. Some of the local people hated him because he had money to rebuild his fortunes, while returning Confederates had only worthless Confederate scrip.

When Jesse Dobbins made his appearance in Yadkinville during court week, the sheriff approached him and stated, "Dobbins, consider yourself under arrest."

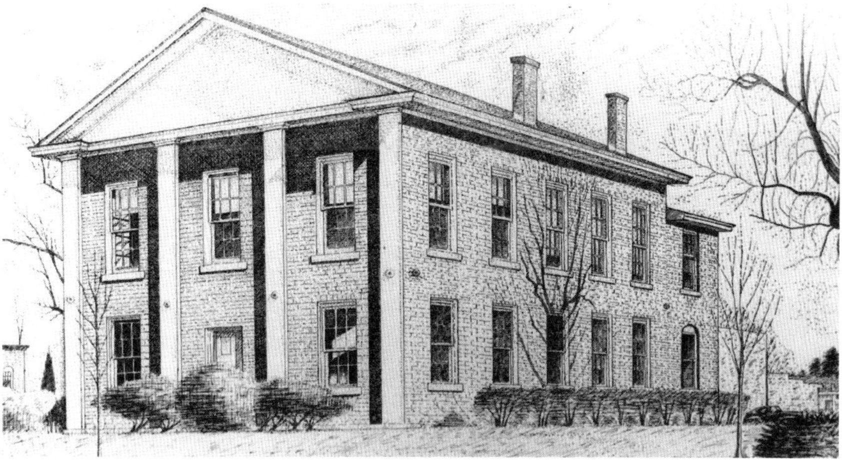

Old Yadkin County courthouse where court records regarding murder charges against Dobbins and the others involved in the shooting were kept. *Danny Casstevens, artist. Collection of Frances H. Casstevens.*

"What is the charge against me?" Jesse asked.

"Murder," replied the sheriff.

With those words, Dobbins made a sudden movement away from the officer and then said, "Sheriff, I have no ill feelings nor bear any malice against you. There have been enough men killed, but before I will submit to arrest on the charge of murder when I was fighting in self-defense, there will be more men killed." Dobbins jumped astride a horse hitched nearby and rode to Salisbury. He knew there was a regiment of Union solders stationed there.

The next day, Dobbins returned to Yadkinville with a troop of Federal soldiers. Jesse, a Union colonel and three private soldiers entered the clerk's office in the courthouse in Yadkinville.

The colonel looked around and asked, "Which one of you is the clerk of this court?"

The clerk replied, "I am. What can I do for you?"

The colonel demanded to know what was going on. "Don't you people know the war is over? Get your old records and burn them," the colonel ordered.

The officer wanted to burn all the records pertaining to the indictment of Dobbins. The clerk quickly gathered the court record books that contained any reference to the murder of Captain West at the Bond School and started to put them in the fireplace to burn. However, the colonel had second thoughts and told the clerk to stop.

"Better save those books for future reference, but you can cancel all the charges of murder against Dobbins and the other conscript."

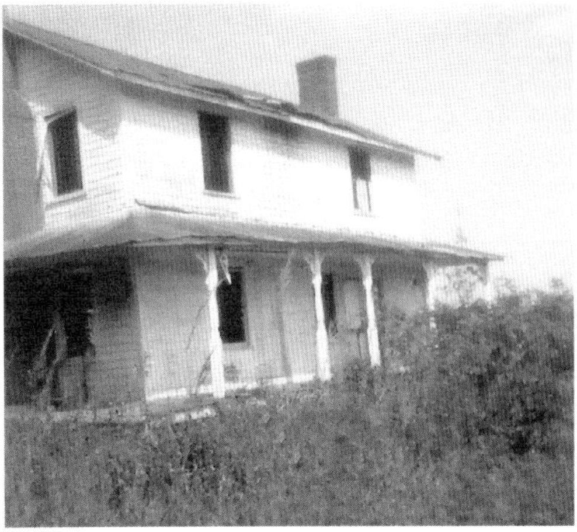

The home of Jesse Dobbins, seen here in the 1970s, is no longer standing. *Photography by Frances H. Casstevens.*

If a trial had been held and the witnesses told the truth, Dobbins would have had a chance to defend himself and he probably would have been cleared of the charge of murder. However, no trial was ever held, and even the documents that named those who had been indicted by the grand jury were hidden for nearly 150 years. Naturally, rumors circulated and subsequent generations wondered what had really happened at the Bond School and who actually killed Captain West.

Whether Dobbins was guilty or not, he and all the men in the schoolhouse were guilty of evading the Confederate conscription laws and of firing on militia officers. A couple of the men were deserters from the Confederate army, and they could have faced either imprisonment or a firing squad for desertion.

Once things settled down, Dobbins tried to live peaceably. Safe from arrest but still under a cloud of suspicion, Jesse had made many enemies because of his actions at the school and because he had joined the Union army. With Yankee dollars in his pocket, he prospered financially from a gristmill and several other business enterprises. He built a large house that stood on Country Club Road until just a few years ago.

DEATH OF JESSE DOBBINS

Dobbins ran the gristmill for a number of years until his death. Until just a few years ago, the ruins of the mill towered over the waters of what local residents call Dobbins's Mill Pond. Jesse Dobbins was found dead one day at his mill. Rumors were rampant that he had been killed by someone who held a grudge against him.

It was true that the fifty-three-year-old Dobbins died while working at the mill, but he was not murdered. His physician, Dr. E.M. Allred, stated that Dobbins had died suddenly of a "paralysis of the brain [stroke] on March 10, 1883." Dr. Allred knew that Dobbins's health had begun to decline in 1879 when he was confined to bed with "inflammatory rheumatism." Dr. Allred had examined Dobbins about a week before his death and found that he was "rapidly losing the use of his left side."

Over the years, the participants in the shootout at the Bond School died, and the facts of the event went to the grave with them. Even though Jesse left an account of the event (written after the war), he made no mention of who had fired the shot that killed Captain West. He did maintain that the conscripts had fired in "self-defense." They believed they had the right to avoid the draft. Even Judge Richmond Pearson believed the Confederate conscript laws were illegal, and he issued writs of habeas corpus that ordered the release of a number of men being held as conscripts.

Fate of the Conscripts

Anderson Douglas later served in Company F, Twenty-eighth Regiment, North Carolina Troops, Confederate States Army, and was wounded at Reams' Station on August 25, 1864. His arm had to be amputated. John "Jackson" Douglas was shot by the Home Guard in the arm and was thus exempt from military service. His brother Sanford remained in hiding until the war had ended.

Hugh Sprinkle served in Company C, Thirtieth Regiment. He was living in Yadkin County with his wife and five children in 1880.

The Willard brothers were part of a large group captured at Birch Mountain while attempting to cross into Tennessee. Also among those captured were Enoch Brown and Horace Allgood. Initially, they were held at Camp Vance near Morganton. Brown and the Willard boys escaped from Camp Vance but were recaptured. Yadkin County officials did not want them back in Yadkin so they were sent to the Forsyth County jail. There, a sister of the Willards helped them escape. Horace Allgood returned to Yadkin County after the war and was living with his wife, according to the 1880 census. Benjamin Willard also returned and was listed in the 1880 census along with Enoch Brown.

Letters from Jesse Dobbins to his family indicated that Thomas Adams, James Caswell Wooten and Robert E. Hutchens had fled with him to Kentucky. Adams witnessed the will made by William Dobbins shortly before his death. James Caswell Wooten returned to Yadkin County where he was listed with his wife and eight children in the 1880 federal census.

An unexpected result of the return of Jesse Dobbins to Yadkin County had major, long-lasting effects. Dobbins and two other Yadkin County men—Dr. Evan Benbow and W.W. Patterson—established the Republican Party in Yadkin County. The county has remained Republican from that time into the twenty-first century.

WHO MURDERED LAURA FOSTER?

Hang down your head, Tom Dooley,
Poor boy, you're bound to die.

No book on crime in North Carolina would be complete without mention of Tom Dula. The former Confederate soldier became famous in the 1960s, one hundred years after his hanging, when the Kingston Trio recorded "Tom Dooley." (See Appendix I for two versions of this song.) Legend says that Tom Dula wrote the words while in prison awaiting his execution. The song was based on the true story of the murder of Dula's alleged bride-to-be, Laura Foster, and the subsequent trial, conviction and execution of Dula for her murder.

Over the years, hundreds of articles have appeared in print and several versions of the ballad of Tom Dooley have been published in folk song anthologies. After the success of the Kingston Trio with their ballad, a motion picture entitled *Legend of Tom Dooley* was released by Columbia Pictures in 1959 starring Michael Landon as Tom.

Tom's story has intrigued readers for over one hundred years and it will continue to do so. A resurgence of interest has been generated by a play based on the book *Tom Dooley: A Wilkes County Legend*, written by Karen Wheeling Reynolds. The play was first performed in 2000 by the Wilkes Playmakers in North Wilkesboro and is now in its sixth season. The Kingston Trio took part in the opening performance of the play on June 23, 2006.

The facts of the story of Thomas Dula and Laura Foster have blended with the fiction and a legend was born.

MAJOR CHARACTERS IN THE TRAGEDY

Thomas C. Dula was born June 20, 1844, to Thomas P. Dula and Mary Keaton. The couple had married in 1822. He was twenty-one years old on May 25, 1866, the supposed date of Laura Foster's murder. Although among the less affluent residents of the Reedy Branch area, Tom was actually the grandnephew of Captain William Dula, the wealthiest land owner in the area called Happy Valley.

A reporter for the *New York Herald,* writing at the time of the murder trial, described Tom while "not handsome, [he] might be called good-looking." Tom was not only attractive but also in great demand to furnish music for the social gatherings in the valley because of his talents with the fiddle.

He was also popular with the local girls around Elkville. They were devastated when Tom enlisted in Company K, Forty-second Regiment as a private. He was soon promoted to musician as a drummer. He was three months shy of his eighteenth birthday. His two brothers had already been killed in the war. Perhaps Tom believed it was his duty to replace his brothers in the fight.

Tom's army record shows that he was confined in a hospital first in Petersburg, Virginia, from November 1 through November 24, for treatment of an unknown ailment. His name appears on a Register of Confederate States Hospital, which contained a list of distributed clothing and accoutrements. He may have contracted malaria since his regiment had seen little fighting until that time. The men spent most of their time on guard duty and drilling on the Virginia coast at City Point near Petersburg.

On December 3, 1862, Dula was confined to the Episcopal Church Hospital in Williamsburg, Virginia, with intermittent fever (probably a recurrence of malaria) and remained there until December 25, when he rejoined his regiment. The Forty-second was assigned to duty along the Blackwater River from Ivor Station on the Norfolk and Petersburg Railroad to Franklin. They were frequently involved in skirmishes with the enemy.

Dula was listed as present but sick on the muster roll for January–February 1863, in which his rank was listed as "musician." The regimental drummer played an important roll in the numerous drills the soldiers practiced daily. Because of their excellence in performing drills, the Forty-second was asked to perform at the funeral of General Archibald Gracie, who was killed during the siege of Petersburg on December 2, 1864.

The Forty-second Regiment arrived in Petersburg on June 17, 1864, to defend the trenches there for the next four months. Subsequent muster rolls show Tom served with Company K of the Forty-second until September–October 1864, when he was noted as absent, having been in a Richmond hospital since August 10, 1864.

There were unsubstantiated rumors that while stationed in Wilmington, North Carolina, Tom had an affair with a married woman and her husband caught them in bed. According to the reporter for the *New York Herald*, some of Tom's ex-military compatriots claimed that he had shot the husband and killed him when the lovers were discovered together.

In March of 1865, the Forty-second Regiment was involved in the fighting near Kinston, North Carolina, where Tom Dula was captured at Wise's Fork on March 10, 1865, and imprisoned by the Federals at Point Lookout, Maryland, on March 16, 1865, where he remained until June 11, 1865.

Point Lookout, established in 1863, was located on a peninsula at the junction of the Potomac River and the Chesapeake Bay in St. Mary's County, Maryland. The few buildings were used as kitchens and mess halls. The prisoners were housed in tents surrounded by a high fence. The prison capacity was 10,000 men, but at one time 22,000 were imprisoned there. In addition to the overcrowding, the food was inadequate, the tents were old and insufficient and the water was bad.

In order to gain his release from the Yankee prison at Point Lookout, Maryland, Tom signed the Oath of Allegiance on June 11, 1865. At that time, he was described as 5 feet 9½ inches tall with dark brown hair and brown eyes. After his release, Tom began the long journey home to his widowed mother's house on Reedy Branch in Wilkes County. He probably walked all the way, as did many other Confederates.

Ann Foster Melton (real name Angeline Pauline Foster or Triplett, sometimes called Anny) was born circa 1843. She was described by John Foster West as a beautiful woman. Although illiterate, she had the "manner and bearing of an accomplished lady, and all the natural poise that would grace a born beauty." Ann (or Anny) was one of several illegitimate children born to Carlotta "Lotty" Foster. Ann was married to James Melton when she was only sixteen, not, as the popular legend goes, during the war while Tom was away fighting. Actually, the couple was married on June 22, 1859—three years before Tom went to war. Whether she and Tom were having an affair before he left is questionable, but it was verified by her mother on the witness stand.

Ann was described by the reporter for the *New York Herald* as "a most beautiful woman." However, in addition to being promiscuous, she was temperamental, demanding, aggressive, lazy and had no interest in household tasks.

A daughter, Martha Jane Melton, was born to Ann and James Melton about 1861. This was before Tom Dula went to war. The *New York Herald* reporter described the community in which the crime occurred as an area where "free-lovism prevails, and it is a wise child that knows his own father." Who actually fathered Martha Jane is questionable.

Ann was confident and also vain. She was reported to have said after the murder, "A rope will never go around this pearly white neck."

Laura Foster, the murder victim, was daughter of Wilson and Martha "Patsy" Bowman Foster. Local legend had it that she was eighteen years old at the time of her death. Her father testified that she was twenty-two, and that she lived with him and her brother James in Caldwell County at German's Hill. The 1860 census record of Buffalo District, Caldwell County, North Carolina, claimed that Laura was seventeen that year, so she would have to have been at least twenty-two or maybe twenty-three when she died. In 1860 Laura was living with her parents and four siblings: James, age eleven; Elbert, age eight; John, age six; and Elizabeth, age two. Neither of her parents could read or write, and her father listed his occupation as a "farmer."

According to one researcher, Laura Foster, the murder victim, may have been a fourth cousin to Ann Triplett Foster Melton. Many of the families in rural North Carolina were (and are) related by blood or marriage and shared the same last names. It is not known when Tom and Laura became acquainted. He may have known her all her life, or he may have met her when he returned from the war. Although her home was in Caldwell County, it was only a few miles from where Tom Dula and Ann Melton lived.

Laura was described as very beautiful, "with chestnut curls and merry blue eyes," but she was also "wild as a buck." The *New York Herald* described Laura as "beautiful but frail." Pauline Foster testified that Laura's teeth were large and that there was "a natural space right in the center of her mouth."

John Foster West wrote, "While growing up in the area, I never heard a word of criticism directed against [Laura] and never heard the slightest hint that she was immoral or diseased, the latter condition resulting directly in her death. Yet, if Laura had syphilis and gave it to Tom, she may have contracted the disease from someone else, thus making her a 'loose woman.'" Pauline "Perline" Foster, Ann's second cousin, had come from Watauga County to work for James and Ann Foster Melton. Her name was often spelled Perline because of the local pronunciation. Pauline's stated purpose was to earn money to get medical treatment for syphilis, which she had acquired in Watauga County. Dr. George N. Carter subsequently treated her with "blue stone, blue mass, and caustic." Pauline would prove to be a key witness in the arrest and trial of Tom Dula, and she was the key witness against him. Her character was so questionable that the *New York Herald* reporter wrote that she was "remarkable for nothing but debasement, and may be dismissed with the statement that she has since married a white man and given birth to a Negro."

James G. Melton, husband of Ann Foster, was a cobbler by trade. He served in the Confederate army from 1861 to 1865. It was James Melton (rather than Tom Dula) who had served in the Twenty-sixth North Carolina—the regiment of which Governor Zeb Vance had once been colonel—enlisting on June 12, 1861, at the age of twenty-three. He was wounded in the shoulder and right leg at Gettysburg in July of 1863. He was wounded again near the end of the war on March 30,

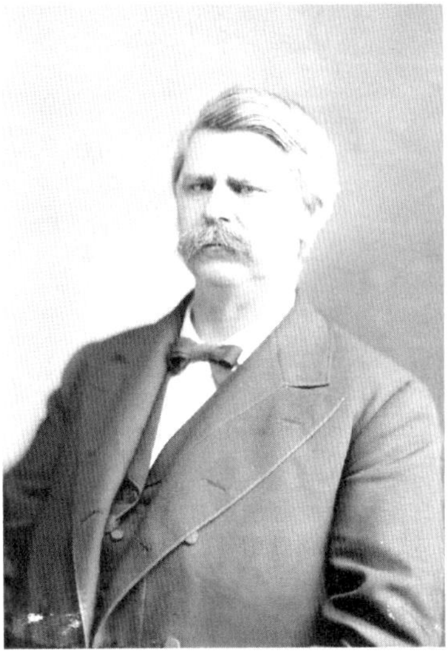

Ex-Governor Zebulon B. Vance, Dula's attorney. *Courtesy of the Library of Congress.*

1865, at Hatcher's Run. He was taken to a hospital at Richmond, Virginia, but when the city fell to the Union forces, Melton was imprisoned at Point Lookout, Maryland. He was released on June 26, 1865, after taking the Oath of Allegiance two weeks after Tom Dula started home from that same prison.

Carlotta "Lotty" Foster, born about 1820, was the mother of Ann Foster Melton and several other illegitimate children. In the 1850 and 1860 censuses, Lotty was listed under the surname Triplett, as were her children. However, during Tom Dula's trial, she was called Lotty Foster and was listed as such in the 1870 Wilkes County census. Some have speculated that she was married or at least lived with a man named Triplett, who abandoned her with one or two children. Foster could have been her maiden name, and when she started using it so did her children; or she may have actually been married to a man named Foster at some time between 1860 and 1870.

Ex-Governor Zebulon Baird Vance, the primary attorney in Dula's two trials, was born in Buncombe County. He attended law school at the University of North Carolina and later practiced law in Asheville. He entered politics at age twenty-eight and was the youngest member ever elected to Congress. He served the Confederate army, initially as a captain in the Rough and Ready Guards, a company of the Fourteenth North Carolina Regiment. Vance was then elected colonel of the Twenty-sixth North Carolina. He served as governor from 1862 to 1865, and again from 1877 to 1879. After the war, Vance was imprisoned in the Old Capitol Prison in Washington, D.C.

EVENTS LEADING UP TO THE MURDER

When he returned home, Tom Dula reportedly resumed his affair with Ann Melton, an affair that may have begun as early 1859, at least three years before he joined the Confederacy in 1862. Tom would have been fifteen years old in 1859. He also began having an affair with Laura Foster in the early months of 1866.

Shortly thereafter on Sunday, May 13, 1866, Tom told a neighbor, R.D. Hall, that he "was diseased," and that he was going to "put through"—or kill—the one who had given it to him. Tom made two trips to visit Laura Foster, the first on Sunday, May 20, the second the following Wednesday, two days before her death. On Thursday, May 24, Ann Melton told Pauline Foster that Tom had given her the "pock" and that he had contracted it from Laura Foster. (Another time, Pauline stated that Ann told her in April.) Ann reportedly said that her husband, James Melton, also had the disease. This is questionable, since James Melton lived a long and happy life and died sometime after 1910. After Ann's death he married Louisa Gilbert.

On the morning of Thursday, May 24, Tom visited Lotty Foster, Ann Melton's mother, to borrow her mattock. He was later seen by Martha Gilbert digging along the path near the branch. This spot turned out to be only about two to three hundred yards from where Laura's grave was discovered.

Tom asked Laura to meet him the next morning so that they could elope. She saddled her horse and, with a small bundle of clothes, she rode out to meet her fate. When Laura did not return, her father and brother searched everywhere for her, and came to the conclusion that she must have eloped with Tom Dula. Three days after her disappearance, Laura's horse came home. His rope halter was worn to shreds, as if he had been tied and had pulled on the rope until he was free. During the search for Laura, the tree was found where the horse had been tethered.

Laura's Body Discovered

Two months passed and one night Ann Foster Melton and Pauline Foster had an argument. The girls were overheard and soon the authorities were notified. Pauline agreed to tell what she knew. She swore that Ann had told her that Tom Dula killed Laura Foster. Pauline also said that she and Ann had gone to a grave near Elkville to see if it had been disturbed. With Pauline's directions, a large search party combed the area and the shallow grave was soon located. The medical examiner was called and determined that Laura had been stabbed in her breast and that her legs had been broken so she would fit in the small grave.

There was no doubt that the body was that of Laura Foster. Her long chestnut brown hair and her gold tooth were enough to positively identify her. This was further substantiated by the homespun dress she wore. The shoes were identified by James Melton, who claimed he had made them for Laura. Her face was covered with an apron, neatly folded four times, as if done by a woman.

Laura's body was placed in a coffin and carried to what is now known as Laura Foster Ridge for burial. Her original tombstone was erroneously inscribed with her date of death as 1865. A more recent plaque has been placed by the Woodmen of the World, Lodge 95, with additional and correct information.

TOM FLEES TO TENNESSEE

Tom Dula was not the only murder suspect. He, along with Jack Adkins, Ben Ferguson, Jack Keaton and several other young men who had been associated with Laura Foster, fled the neighborhood.

Tom changed his name to Tom Hall and went to Johnson County, Tennessee. There, he obtained employment from Colonel James W.M. Grayson. Grayson was a prominent citizen who had served in the Federal Fourth Tennessee Infantry as a lieutenant colonel, then as a major. Tom worked for Grayson just long enough to buy a pair of boots and left just before the Wilkes County sheriff arrived at the Grayson home. Colonel Grayson led the officers along the trail Tom had taken, and they soon found him. Grayson told Tom he was under arrest and Tom surrendered. Then Grayson put Tom Dula on his horse and they rode back to the town of Trade. The next morning, the Wilkes County officers, with Dula still riding behind Grayson, rode back to Wilkesboro. The capture took place about nine miles west of Mountain City, Tennessee, on July 10, 1866.

Contrary to standard procedures, Tom Dula was arrested before there was any hard evidence that a crime had been committed and before the body was actually found. He was extradited illegally from Tennessee without the proper papers.

Tom was taken to Wilkesboro and jailed. The next day, Ann Melton was also arrested. However, Jack Keaton, who was also under suspicion, had an alibi and was released. Tom and Ann were bound over until the fall term of court.

Ex-Governor Zebulon B. Vance announced he would defend Tom because the accused man had been a Confederate soldier. He may have believed that Tom had served in the Twenty-sixth Regiment, when in fact, he served in Company K, Forty-second Regiment, North Carolina Troops. James Melton, however, had served in the Twenty-sixth Regiment.

Vance was assisted by Attorney Robert Franklin Armfield, a lawyer who had practiced in Yadkin County before the Civil War. Armfield had served with the Twenty-eighth Regiment, North Carolina Troops. Armfield began his practice in Yadkinville, but later moved to Statesville. He had plenty of trial experience, having served as state solicitor for the Sixth District in 1862 while on furlough from the Confederate army. He later served in the state Senate in 1874–75.

FIRST TRIAL

There was much hard feeling against Tom in Wilkesboro and, in order to get a fair trial, Vance requested the trial be moved to Statesville. The handwritten transcript (not verbatim, but more of a summary) of the testimony at the trial has been deciphered and included in John Foster West's book, *Lift Up Your Head, Tom Dooley*.

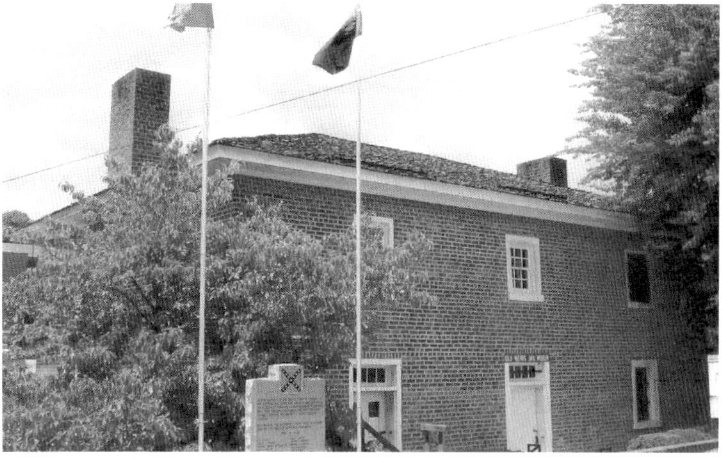

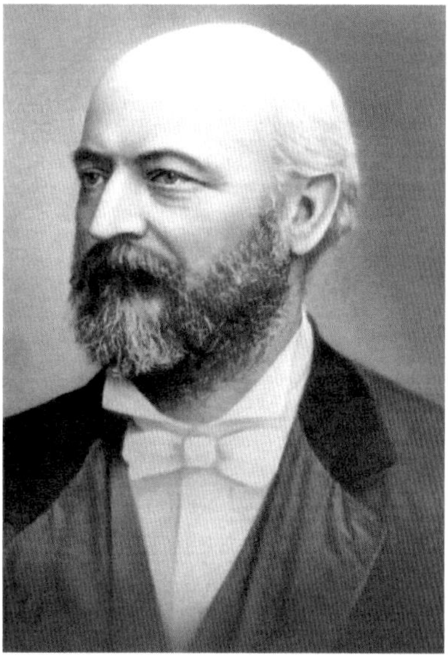

Above: Old Wilkes County jail where Tom Dula and Ann Melton were initially held. *Courtesy of Greg Cheek.*

Right: Attorney Robert Armfield assisted in the first trial but not the second. *Collection of Frances H. Casstevens.*

A number of witnesses took the stand. Colonel James M. Isbell presented a crude map of the neighborhood around the site of Laura Foster's grave.

Wilson Foster (Laura's father) testified that she left his house early one Friday morning in May. He also testified that Tom Dula often came to see Laura and sometimes he spent the night. In the week before the murder, Tom had visited Laura on Sunday and again on Wednesday, two days before she disappeared. Laura had taken a horse with a shoe that was easily identified. He followed the tracks to the Bates place and then lost the trail. At the James Melton home, he found that Melton's wife, Ann, was still in bed. Wilson testified that the horse returned home the next morning. The rope attached to her halter had been broken. Nearly four weeks later, Wilson Foster found the rest of the rope tied to a dogwood tree at the Bates place. After Laura's body was found, Wilson identified her by a hole in the shoes she wore, which had been made by James Melton, the local cobbler. He also recognized her clothes. Wilson also stated that before she left home, Laura "had boils about her shoulder." Wilson had been quoted by some that he would kill Laura if he found her, a statement he denied making.

Mrs. Betsy Scott testified that she had talked to Laura on the day she disappeared. Laura had told her she was going to meet Tom Dula at the Bates place. Carl Carlton testified that he saw Tom Dula on the path that went through his yard to the Bates place. The time was early in the morning, just a little after sunup. Tom asked Carlton if the path led to Hezekiah Kendall's house. Hezekiah Kendall testified that he saw Tom about eight o'clock between his place and Carlton's, headed toward the Bates place. When Kendall asked Tom if he had been out with a woman, the prisoner replied, "No, I have quit that."

Mrs. James Scott then testified that Tom had come to her house and asked to see her brother, James Anderson. The time was "after breakfast." Tom waited a few minutes, then walked toward the home of James and Ann Foster Melton.

The longest and the most damaging testimony was given by Pauline Foster. She claimed that on Thursday, the day before Laura disappeared, Tom had asked her for some alum because he had a sore in his mouth. He also wanted to borrow a canteen. Pauline loaned him one, which he took to Carson McGuire to fill with moonshine liquor.

Pauline Foster also testified that the defendant often stayed at the Melton home overnight, and that James and Ann Melton slept in separate beds. She also testified that after James had gone to sleep, Tom would slip into Ann's bed. Pauline said that Ann Melton had contracted the "pock" (syphilis) from Tom Dula. On Friday, according to Pauline, Ann was absent from the house until about an hour before daylight, and when she returned, her dress and shoes were wet. Ann got in the bed with Pauline and remained until most of the day. Pauline also said that she returned to the house that Friday (the day Laura was believed to have been murdered) and found Tom Dula standing beside the bed talking to Ann. The most damaging testimony was that when Ann asked him if he had run away with Laura Foster, Tom replied, "I have no use for Laura Foster," and laughed. He did not remain long after that.

Pauline testified that Tom left for Tennessee about four weeks after Laura disappeared. He came to the Melton house to say goodbye to Ann. This was two or three days after James Melton said within Tom's hearing that the Hendrickses were saying that Tom had killed Laura. Tom laughed and said, "They would have it to prove and perhaps take a beating besides." Pauline also stated that Tom told her that they were telling lies on him and he had to leave the area. She described how Tom and Ann embraced and how he promised to return for her and his widowed mother at Christmas.

When cross-examined, Pauline stated that Tom had been at the Melton house between eight and nine o'clock. She stated that she and James Melton, for whom she worked, planted corn all day, while Ann remained in bed.

Damaging testimony was presented by Lotty Foster, the mother of Ann Foster Melton. She testified that Tom had asked to borrow a mattock and that it was not returned for three or four days. She had to ask for it twice before getting it back. She also testified about the affair between her daughter and the prisoner. She stated that two years before the war (1859 or 1860), she caught Tom Dula in bed with her daughter, who was already married at the time. He jumped out and got under the bed. She ordered him out of the house and he left with his clothes off. Tom objected to her statement.

Another witness, Martha Gilbert, testified that she saw Tom Dula using the mattock on the road between Mrs. Dula's and Lotty Foster's. She asked what he was doing and he said he was "fixing the path and making the road wider" so he could travel it at night. The place where he was digging was only two hundred to three hundred yards from Laura's shallow grave.

Dr. George N. Carter testified that in March or April of 1866, he treated Tom Dula for syphilis. Tom told the doctor that he had gotten the disease from Laura Foster. Dr. Carter had also examined the body of the victim and found that she had been stabbed by a knife in the left breast between the third and fourth ribs. The grave was only 2½ feet deep, very narrow and not long enough for the body. The body was badly decomposed.

Some of the most damning testimony was the statement by R.D. Hall that Tom had told him he "was going to put them through who diseased him."

Mrs. James Scott testified about the fight between Pauline Foster and Ann Foster Melton, which had occurred in her yard. Pauline had gone to help Mrs. Scott when Ann accosted her. They fought over remarks that Pauline had made earlier (in jest, she claimed) that she and Tom had killed Laura Foster. Mrs. Scott testified that Pauline had said, "It is the truth and you are as deep in the mud as I am in mire." Ann replied, "You are a liar!" Then Ann confronted Pauline about having the disease, and Pauline replied, "Yes, we all have it!"

J.W. Winkler stated he heard Pauline say, "I would swear a lie any time for Tom Dula, wouldn't you, George?" She may also have told lies about Dula's part in the murder, perhaps out of jealousy, perhaps to cover herself.

Washington Anderson stated that all three—Ann, Pauline and Tom—were engaging in illicit sex. He recalled seeing Pauline Foster meet Tom Dula one night near the road. He also testified that she spent the night with Tom in the woods and that Anderson was with them.

Throughout the trial, Tom always maintained he was innocent and refused to implicate anyone. In his defense, Attorney Vance portrayed Laura Foster as a woman of loose morals and Tom as a brave soldier who had been seduced by her. Testimony by others, however, may have led the jury to believe that Tom had no morals at all. The jury found Tom guilty. Vance appealed to the state supreme court and Tom was granted a new trial.

THE SECOND TRIAL

The second trial took place in January of 1868. At the close of the second trial, after all the testimony had been heard, Judge William M. Shipp summarized the facts of the case and, in doing so, sealed the fate of Tom Dula. Again, Dula was found guilty. Another appeal was made but no new trial was granted. The guilty verdict of the second trial stood, and the hanging was scheduled for May 1, 1868.

Governor Vance was assisted by Richard M. Allison, who had also aided in the first trial. Allison, a former Confederate cavalry officer, was from a prominent Iredell County family. David Moffat Furches of Davie County assisted in the second trial. He had studied law under Chief Justice Richmond Pearson.

Attorney R.F. Armfield was unable to assist in the second trial. It was rumored that when he arrived, Dula had already been tried and convicted.

THE HANGING

On his way to his hanging, legend says that Tom Dula sat upon his coffin and played a tune on his fiddle to entertain the large crowd that attended the event. When the noose was placed around Tom's neck, he reportedly laughed and said, "I'd a washed my neck, if I'd known you were going to use such a nice clean rope."

When asked if he had any last words to say, Tom grew serious and asked, "Gentlemen, do you see this hand? Does it tremble?" Then he boldly declared, "I never hurt a hair on the girl's head."

After talking for nearly an hour, at 2:24 p.m., the cart on which Tom stood was moved, and his body was suspended in air. The fall was only about two feet and his neck was not broken. He continued to breathe for about five minutes, but did not struggle. After twenty minutes, the body was cut down. If he had not lived with honor, since he had shot one irate husband, been in many sexual relationships outside of marriage and was possibly the murderer or an accomplice in the death of Laura Foster, Tom certainly died with dignity as he swung from the noose.

The body of Thomas Dula was carried to the family cemetery near Ferguson. The story was of such national interest that a three-column article was published by the *New York Herald* on May 2, 1868.

Because their trials had been separated, Ann Melton would not be tried until the courts finished with Tom. Thus, she spent two years in jail. When she did come to trial, she was acquitted because of a confession Tom penned the night before he was hanged. Although Ann escaped the hangman, according to popular legend, she died from injuries she received when an oxcart overturned. Some said, "Satan had come and got her."

Recently Discovered Evidence

Some speculate Ann Melton had killed Laura out of jealousy and that she persuaded Tom to help her bury the body. An undated paper was found in the state archives that appear to be notes taken during Pauline Foster's testimony. Included in the notes is the statement by Pauline that on Saturday morning (after the death of Laura), Ann Melton told her that she'd accomplished what she said she would do. Ann reportedly told Pauline that she had killed Laura Foster and then began cursing about having the venereal disease. Also in the notes were Pauline's statements about going to the site of the grave with Ann Melton.

Pauline's careless statement made to Ben Ferguson—"Yes, Tom and I did kill Laura"—helped convict Tom. After Laura's death, Pauline fled to her home to Watauga County. Whether it was true or not, her statement was enough to get all three of them arrested. Pauline somehow managed to convince the authorities that she was not involved in the killing and she agreed to testify against the other two.

Others who lived in the vicinity were convinced that Ann Melton had committed the actual murder. One story that circulated was related in a letter written on April 24, 1948, by Mrs. Orene West Burrell to her brother, John Foster West. Mrs. Burrell had heard that Laura and Tom had planned to marry and as they rode off on Laura's horse, the "other woman [Ann Foster Melton] stepped out and stabbed her in the side." Mrs. Burrell also recalled hearing her grandma "tell it a hundred times, that you could hear meat frying and see black cats running up and down the walls of the room in which she [Ann Foster Melton] was dying."

Errors Perpetuated

Lies were told by witnesses and errors were made in both of the trials that led to Dula's execution. The trial transcripts testify to the conflicting evidence, hearsay evidence and lack of evidence, combined with circumstantial evidence, which led to a guilty verdict. That verdict was based primarily on circumstantial evidence. No exact date of death for Laura Foster was brought out at the trial. Errors and discrepancies appeared in the contemporary newspapers as well as the later books and articles of dates of Tom's trials or the date that he was actually executed.

Errors regarding the murder of Laura Foster and the trial and conviction of Tom Dula have inadvertently crept into published histories written by reputable authors. Judge Johnson J. Hayes made several errors in the account he included in his history of Wilkes County. He wrote that Laura disappeared in January 1866, while the murder occurred in May. He also noted that Vance had defended Tom because of his love for the men of the Sixteenth North Carolina Regiment. (Vance's regiment was the Twenty-sixth and Vance learned after he accepted the job that Dula had served not with the Twenty-sixth but with the Forty-second.) Judge Hayes attributes the song to T.C. Land, rather than Tom Dula. Even well-educated men who try to be meticulous with setting down the facts can err, as is evident here. Louis H. Manarin, in Volume Ten of *North Carolina Troops, 1861–1865,* also erred in stating that Dula was executed in 1866.

There is even disagreement as to the day that Laura was supposedly murdered. A recent feature article in the *Winston-Salem Journal* states that Laura was believed to have died May 28, 1866. That day would have been a Monday. Everyone who testified said that Laura left home on Friday morning to meet her lover and was never seen again. That date would have been Friday, May 25, 1866.

Even the date of Tom's hanging is incorrect on his tombstone:

TOM DULA

HANGED MAY 1, 1866

FOR THE MURDER OF

LAURA FOSTER.

Tom Dula's grave, marked by a large tombstone, stands on a bluff overlooking a creek. Since the Kingston Trio's recording, the site has been visited by thousands of curiosity seekers. Some have carried away pieces of his tombstone. It seems there is no rest for poor Tom anywhere on earth. If Tom were alive, he would surely "hang down his head and cry" at the desecration of his tombstone.

ATTEMPT TO SET THE RECORD STRAIGHT

In the closing years of the twentieth century, Ken Welborn, publisher of the *North Wilkesboro Record*, Karen Wheeling Sloop Reynolds and Sandra Watts did extensive research into the two trials of Tom Dula. They found that the presiding judge was asked to omit testimony, that the state presented only circumstantial evidence and that the testimony of Pauline Foster, the main witness for the prosecution, was unreliable. Pauline had also been arrested as a co-conspirator but released when she agreed to testify against Dula.

Out of that research, Karen Wheeling Reynolds brought all the characters in this tragedy to life with her book *Tom Dooley: A Wilkes County Legend*. The book seems to implicate Pauline Foster and perhaps Jack Keaton as the most likely suspects.

Petition for a Pardon

The *North Wilkesboro Record* ran a series of articles about the murder that coincided with the opening of a play about the Tom Dula story. Ken Welborn employed a team of lawyers from North Wilkesboro to prepare a petition to present to the governor of North Carolina asking for a pardon for Thomas C. Dula. Welborn claimed that Dula's confession was written to save Ann from hanging and was not a true confession of guilt.

The way in which Thomas Dula was arrested and the manner in which his trials were conducted have been studied and analyzed by Attorney Ted G. West of Lenoir, North Carolina. West concluded that if Tom Dula had been arrested today and the same evidence was submitted as during his actual trial, it seems more than likely that his conviction would have been set aside due to insufficient evidence. He was extradited from Tennessee illegally and he was convicted on circumstantial evidence alone.

Dula Immortalized in Song

The first recorded version of a song about the Laura Foster murder was by Grayson and Whittier in 1929. Frank Warner, a folklorist, recorded it in 1952. He had heard the song from Frank Profitt in 1940 and passed it to Alan Lomax, who published it in *Folk Song: USA*. However, it was the Kingston Trio's 1957 recording that gained national recognition and for which the Trio won their first Grammy Award. Since that time, Doc Watson (the blind guitarist and singer from Wilkes County) expanded the scope of the song in his version. Several other bluegrass bands have recorded the story of Tom Dula over the years. John A. Lomax's version of "Tom Dooley" was included in 1959 on Jim Ed Brown's album *Country's Best on Record*. It was also on an album entitled *Tom Paley, John Cohen, and Mike Seeger Sing Songs of the New Lost City Ramblers*. The Tom Dooley String Band, which performs in the play in Wilkes County, hopes to have their version recorded in 2006.

In 2001 the recording of "Tom Dooley" by the Kingston Trio was included in a list of "Songs of the Century." This listing was sponsored by the Recording Industry Association of America, the National Endowment for the Arts and Scholastic to "promote a better understanding of America's musical and cultural heritage."

TOM DOOLEY MUSEUM

Many tourists visit the graves of Laura Foster and Ann Melton each year. The grave of Tom Dula is on private property and is not accessible to the public. However, the Tom Dooley Museum is located in Ferguson at the Whippoorwill Academy and Village at Ferguson. Interested persons may also visit the Old Wilkes Jail where Tom was incarcerated before being moved to Statesville.

UNANSWERED QUESTIONS

What motive did Tom have to kill Laura? Was it because she had given him syphilis? Or was it because she was pregnant and he did not want to marry her?

Did Ann kill Laura because she was jealous? Did she learn that Tom and Laura planned to elope and committed murder to prevent the marriage? Once the deed was done, did Ann seek Tom's help in covering up the crime and in burying the body? Why was the grave too small? Was the crime premeditated and was the grave dug ahead of time?

There was actually no evidence to definitely place the blame for Laura Foster's death on Tom Dula. In fact, the jealousy of Pauline Foster and Ann Foster Melton seem to be greater motivating factors. Pauline may have enlisted the help of Jack Keaton to kill her rival, Laura Foster. Ann Melton may have killed her alone or with the help of her mother.

Someone else, perhaps Ann, could have taken the mattock and dug the shallow grave in which the body of Laura Foster was placed. Surely, a man who had served three years in the Confederate army would have been able to dig a grave big enough in which to place a body and to dig it deep enough to avoid detection.

At the party the night before the murder, did someone drug Tom so that he was late in getting up and missed his rendezvous with Laura? Any of the people at Lotty Foster's house that night could have committed the crime. All had motives.

Was Laura Foster killed by a spurned lover? Why did Jack Keaton leave the area so soon after the murder? Was he involved?

Was Tom the victim of anti-Confederate sentiments? Was he blamed by an irate husband (James Melton) for having an affair with the man's wife?

Did Pauline Foster seek her revenge on Tom and Ann because Tom had rejected her advances?

Could the murder of Laura Foster have been committed by Pauline and James Melton? Melton adored his wife and would do anything to make her happy. If he knew that Ann was upset by the thoughts of Tom marrying Laura, perhaps he acted to save her pain and heartbreak.

If syphilis was the motive for the murder, then who gave it to whom? Tom reportedly said he got it from Laura Foster. Yet Pauline was the first person known to have had the disease. She was already infected when she arrived in Wilkes County. Pauline was quoted as saying about the disease, "Yes, we all have it," meaning herself, Ann and Tom Dula along with Laura Foster. Pauline is the first one known to have been treated in March of 1866, soon after she arrived in Wilkes County. Shortly thereafter, Tom was treated by Dr. Carter. Could Tom have contracted the disease from Pauline and passed it on to Ann and Laura? If so, and if the disease was the motive for the murder, the wrong woman was killed. John Foster West agrees with this theory of how the disease was transmitted, with Pauline being the primary source. However, Tom told Dr. Carter that he had caught the disease from Laura Foster. Why?

The Progression of Syphilis

The primary stage of the disease begins with a painless sore or chancre on the sex organs, fingers, lips or tongue ten to thirty days after contact. The secondary state can develop in six to twelve weeks after the chancre. It is evident by a rash on the palms and soles of the feet, aches, sore throat, hair loss and enlarged lymph nodes. There can also be a latent stage in which no physical signs exist for months or even for a lifetime. The late stage of syphilis develops three to four years after contact and is evident by tumors on the skin, bones, liver, central nervous system disorders and eventually dementia or psychosis. Since no symptoms were given for any of the people in this case, it is impossible to determine in which stage of the disease they were or if they even had this particular venereal disease.

Most people who have heard the story do not believe (or do not want to believe) that the handsome courageous soldier Tom Dula committed the crime. Some believe Ann Foster Melton did it; others believe Ann together with Pauline Foster killed Laura Foster.

The unsolved mysteries in this case continue to intrigue us. The story has gained a place in the folklore and legends of our state and nation. Can we believe Tom's last words, spoken from the gallows, when he said that many of the statements made at the trial were false? He continued to deny his guilt and

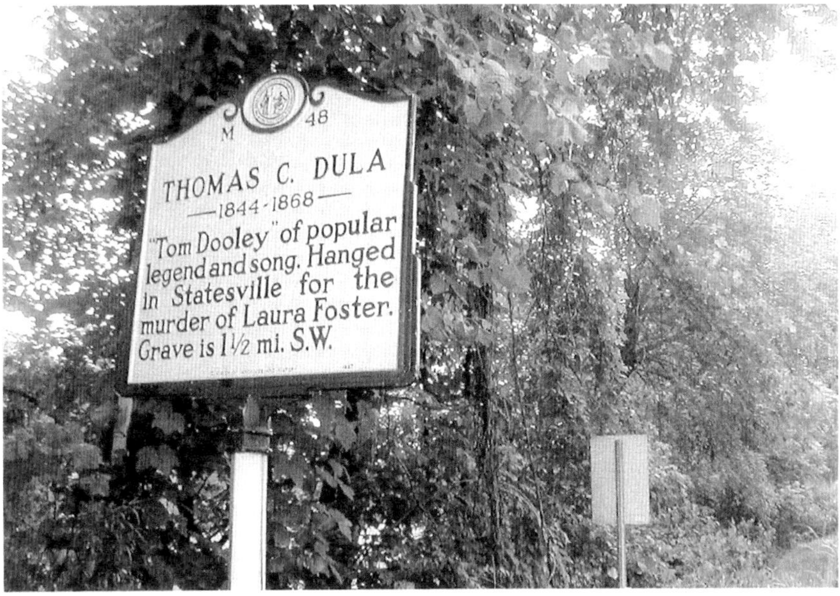

Marker on Highway 268 notes the hanging of Tom "Dooley." *Photography by Frances H. Casstevens.*

reportedly said, "Gentlemen, do you see this hand? I didn't harm a hair on the girl's head." Was this cryptic statement true because the victim was not hit on the head but stabbed in the chest? Or should we believe Tom's handwritten statement that he gave to his solicitor the night before his hanging in which he declared he was "the only person that had any hand in the murder of Laura Foster"? With this note, Tom assumed all the blame for the murder and absolved Ann from any part in the crime. Was this the truth or did he write it because of his undying love for Ann Foster Melton?

It is indeed tragic that Tom Dula survived the war and a Yankee prison only to die three years later at the end of a hangman's noose. It is also tragic that the young girl, Laura Foster, and her unborn child were brutally murdered. The truth of the matter will never be known. There remain many unanswered questions in this case that modern forensic and criminal procedures could have revealed about the perpetrator or perpetrators of the crime.

Who Shot Will Kelly?

I'll never let you marry Will. I'll see him in his grave.

When I was a little girl, I often rode with my father to Huntsville, the oldest settlement in Yadkin County, which had grown up around the famous Shallow Ford of the Yadkin River. Sometimes we drove on to the little community of Farmington in Davie County. In doing so, we passed a deserted two-story antebellum house that sat majestically on a rise on the east side of the road. The overgrown front yard could not hide the walkway still bordered by huge English boxwoods. After one hundred years, it was still a beautiful house and I begged my father to buy it for me so that we could save it from further deterioration. He probably would have bought it but the house was not for sale.

As I grew older I learned of the tragedies that had occurred at the mansion and that it had once been very beautiful inside as well with ornate plasterwork on the ceilings of the rooms. I was intrigued by the stories of the tragedies that had occurred there, especially the story of the murder of Will Kelly.

View of the Crime

The scene Daisy Hunt saw unfolding below from the upstairs window of her spacious bedroom was like a horrible nightmare, only it was really happening. She saw her lover fall to the ground in the barnyard. She could not go to comfort him because her mother had locked her bedroom door, so she watched helplessly as his life's blood stained the new-fallen snow.

Two young lovers—Daisy Hunt and Will Kelly—were doomed from the start. Events were set in motion long before their births that tainted their love affair. Although Daisy and Will lived within a mile of each other, their social classes and economic backgrounds were miles apart. The young couple found themselves in a situation in which wealth, social standing and ancestral bloodlines prevented their happiness and were contributing factors that resulted in the murder of Will Kelly.

Daisy's parents were Dr. Leander G. Hunt (1837–1896) and his wife, Mary "Molly" Martin (1852–1935). Dr. Hunt's father was one of Huntsville's most prominent residents and a descendant of the town's founder, Charles Hunt.

Molly Martin's family was considered the elite upper class of Yadkin River valley. Her mother, Anne Clingman Poindexter, daughter of Francis Anderson Poindexter, was a descendant of Captain Thomas Poindexter and his wife, Betty Pledge (both of whom were recognized by the Daughters of the American Revolution for their service). Francis Anderson Poindexter was the brother of Anne and Jane Poindexter, sisters who married brothers Peter and Jacob Clingman.

Miss Molly Martin grew up in the famous White House, in which Brigadier General Thomas Lanier Clingman spent his childhood living with his uncle Peter Clingman. Molly was accustomed to the wealth and privilege afforded members of her class. Her father owned land, slaves and several businesses in the town of Huntsville. The town was rumored to have been considered as the new state capital (but no documentation has ever been found to support this legend). In the 1860 census, Mary was living with her merchant father, Thomas S. Martin, and her mother, Nancy A., who was listed as a "lady." Also listed in the household were two older brothers, a sister and a younger brother, William A. Martin, age three. He would play a significant part in the unfolding tragedy.

As a young lady, Molly often visited with her Puryear cousins across the river at the Shallow Ford Plantation. One of her cousins, Sarah Ellen Puryear, had extrasensory powers and enjoyed playing parlor games, which included "spirit writing" and "table walking" or "table rapping." This popular parlor game was played by having a group of people sit around a table with their hands along the edges and their fingers touching to make an unbroken circle around the table. Each participant remained silent and concentrated until the table began to move. Then all except Sarah Ellen removed their hands while she kept the tip of one finger touching the top of the table. When questions to the table were posed, the answers were received by counting the raps the table made. The raps were counted and their number corresponded to a letter of the alphabet; for example, three raps equaled the letter *C*.

During one session of table rapping, Molly Martin joined in. Since young girls are usually curious about their future husbands, Sarah Ellen asked the table whom Molly would marry. The answer came back as "L.G. Hunt." At the time, Leander Gwyn Hunt was a medical student. He was well liked but not handsome and was not considered an especially good catch for a young lady. Molly shook her head and said, "It will be a long time before I would think of marrying that moon-faced baboon." However, as time passed, the young doctor returned to Huntsville to practice and he and Molly Hunt were married on the date specified by the table (Sarah Ellen always wrote the information given by the table down) in February of 1879. The groom was forty-one; the bride, only twenty-seven. The newlyweds would soon make their home in the Dalton house.

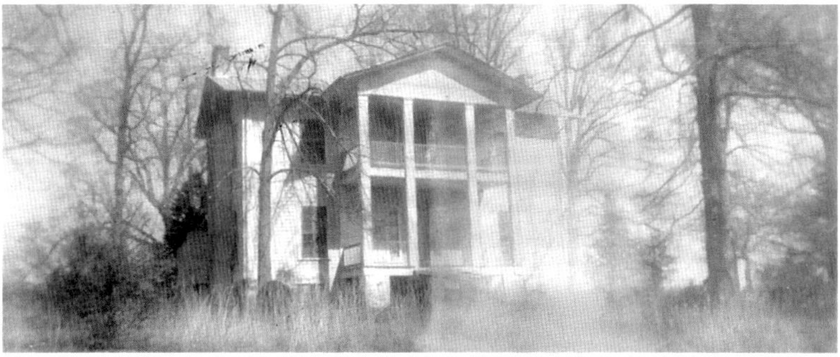

Dalton-Hunt house. Will Kelly was murdered in a nearby barnyard. *Photography by Frances H. Casstevens.*

The Dalton House

The Dalton house was built around 1855 for Mrs. Sarah Byrd Dalton. The Greek Revival–style house had six large rooms, each twenty by thirty feet with twelve-foot-high ceilings. The walls were plastered and painted in a "vari-colored plaster" with unusual colors. The weatherboarded house rose high from the ground and the basement windows could be seen beneath the two-tier porch. On the front of the house, railed porches graced both the first and second floors. Surrounding the house were a number of slave cabins and a large barn sat across a drive that turned off the Farmington Road.

In 1839 Henry Gorman, a plasterer, married Julia Dalton, Sarah Dalton's daughter. The young couple lived with the bride's widowed mother. When the house was being built, Henry (with a crew of slaves to assist him) probably did the work that resulted in the ornate plaster rosettes on the ceilings of the house.

Mystery and scandal have been associated with all of the occupants of the antebellum mansion. There were rumors that Mrs. Sarah Dalton's husband, Jonathan Dalton, was shot by an irate husband who found that Dalton was having an affair with his wife. Another version is that Jonathan Dalton, remembered only as a "traveling man" (he may have been a slave trader), came home to find his wife in bed with another man. Without hesitation, Dalton shot the man and subsequently left the county, never to return. Surry County court records confirm that Dalton was dead by 1825.

House Scarred by Tragic Deaths

The Gormans also suffered a great tragedy. Their little boy, Paul, died in 1858 when he was only four years old. He was reportedly a precocious child who could recite whole chapters from the Bible. He was pampered and petted until

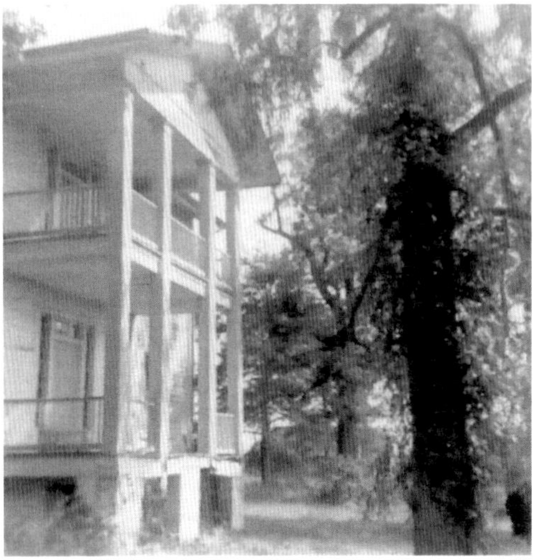

Balcony from which Julia Dalton Gorman reportedly jumped to her death. *Photography by Frances H. Casstevens.*

the family doctor suggested that the boy needed more exercise. His doting grandmother and his mother would not allow his little feet to touch the ground, and for exercise, they had a slave drive the boy up and down the drive in a buggy.

Shortly after the death of the child, Julia's husband died. The loss of both husband and child were too much for her and she reportedly went insane. There were stories that she would sit unclothed for hours on the upper balcony and curse everyone who passed by on the road. Two years after the death of the little boy, Julia was listed as "diseased" on the 1860 census.

According to local lore, Julia Dalton Gorman eventually killed herself. She was said to have climbed over the railings of the balcony and jumped to the ground, where she was impaled on a stake used to tether a cow. Others said she hanged herself. Since there were no death certificates until 1913, the cause of her death is impossible to verify. It can be determined that she died sometime between 1870 and 1880, according to census records.

Tragedy continued to cast a shadow over the beautiful house.

THE DALTON-HUNT HOUSE TRAGEDY

In 1880, a year after his marriage, Dr. Hunt bought the Dalton house from the administrator of Mrs. Dalton's estate. Dr. Hunt and his wife had only one child, a daughter named Daisy. Legends say that she was a beautiful young lady, but residents of Huntsville who knew her said she was not very attractive, but had a long, mule-like face. Perhaps Daisy resembled her father, whom her mother had once called a "moon-faced baboon."

Born in 1882, Daisy was the apple of her father's eye and was sent to be educated at Salem Academy. When she was fourteen years old, Daisy's idyllic life was shattered by the death of her father in 1896. Mrs. Hunt and Daisy continued to live in the mansion. A local boy, Will Kelly, was hired to care for the horses and do other jobs on the plantation. Kelly, born in 1871, was ten years older than the lonely young daughter of his employer.

Unfortunately, Will Kelly was also the illegitimate son of Julia Kelly, who was known to have had at least three illegitimate children. Therefore, Will Kelly would not have been considered by the aristocratic Mrs. Molly Hunt as a suitable suitor for her daughter. However, he and Daisy began a clandestine affair that would have fatal consequences.

One wintry day, Will sent a note by Joe Kimbrough, a former slave who was also employed by Mrs. Hunt, asking Daisy to meet him in the barn. Daisy never received the note. It was intercepted by Mrs. Hunt and instead of Daisy, someone else met Will Kelly that snowy morn on Groundhog Day of 1902. Did Will just want to see Daisy or had they made plans to elope? The contents of the note were never revealed by Mrs. Hunt.

In her room upstairs in the house, Daisy heard gunshots. She ran to the window and looked outside. To her horror, she saw her lover lying on the ground, his blood and brains splattered on a large snow-covered area in front of the barn. Daisy also saw her mother and her uncle, William Martin, standing in the barnyard near the body.

It was always said by the local people that the sight of her lover dying in the bloodstained snow was enough to mark the child she carried.

No one ever knew just who pulled the trigger of the gun that killed Will Kelly. The sheriff was notified, but because of the inclement weather, it was the next day before he arrived on the scene.

After Sheriff Isaac Shore reached the scene of the crime, just south of Huntsville, he sent for the county coroner, J.F. Apperson. The coroner ordered an autopsy to be performed by Bill James, who lived a few miles away in Farmington. James sawed Kelly's head open in search of a bullet.

Everyone assumed that Will Martin had shot Kelly. Martin, Mrs. Hunt's forty-five-year-old brother, was reported to have left the state to seek refuge in Texas. Some sources said he only went as far as Missouri and after a few years returned to Yadkin County. Others maintained that Martin never left at all but remained in hiding in the area for some time.

A posse was organized, composed of every man in the town of Huntsville. However, the posse did not search very thoroughly because the general consensus was that Mrs. Molly Hunt had done the foul deed.

After some time, the search was called off. An inquest into the murder was held at the courthouse in Yadkinville, behind closed doors because of the prominence of the Hunt and Martin families. Joe Kimbrough was called to testify. Joe swore that he had been in the barn feeding the livestock that morning when Kelly arrived to get an answer from his note to Daisy. William Martin was in the barn waiting for Kelly. Kimbrough stated that as Kelly approached the barn, Martin shot him with a pistol. He then described how Kelly, badly wounded, staggered backward toward the gate. But Mrs. Molly Hunt, dressed in the black mourning clothes she had worn since the death of her husband, blocked Kelly's way. Kimbrough testified that the wounded man then turned toward the barnyard well and that another shot was fired. This time, Kelly fell to the ground, bleeding profusely. Martin walked over to Kelly and fired a third and fatal shot into the back of the dying man's head.

No record exists of the verdict reached at the inquest. However, at the next term of Yadkin Superior Court, the grand jury found a true bill against William Martin for the murder of Will Kelly. The next year, 1903, an alias capias was issued for Martin.

The case remained open and even old Joe Kimbrough did not come away unscathed. Even though Joe had cooperated with authorities and testified before the grand jury, he barely escaped being indicted. Solicitor W.C. Hammer sent a bill to the grand jury on October 21, 1903, which charged Kimbrough with harboring William Martin and with aiding and abetting in the murder. However, both bills were returned by the jury as "not a true bill."

Years later, Kimbrough recalled that "Mister Will Martin" was a fine horseman who could put his left hand on the saddle and jump completely over the horse. However, after "he had shot Will Kelly, he [Martin] could not even get up on his horse." Joe remembered that after Martin had tried three times to mount, Joe finally had to help him. The testimony of the black man seemed to place the blame on William Martin. However, for years, rumors persisted that it was really Mrs. Molly Hunt who had fired the gun. Perhaps they both fired.

The story does not end here. Later that year, Daisy Hunt, at age twenty, gave birth to a son. He was named Joseph Cabell Hunt but was always called "Jack." The fatherless child had two strikes against him at the moment of his birth—he was illegitimate and he had a genetic disease that was characterized by dry, thickened and scaling skin (which may have been ichthyosis). Those who knew him said Jack had no sweat or oil glands. His skin had the look of fish scales, and it was prone to bleeding and flaking.

While many believed that Jack had been marked by the bloody scene witnessed by his mother before his birth, others believed that the sins of the fathers had

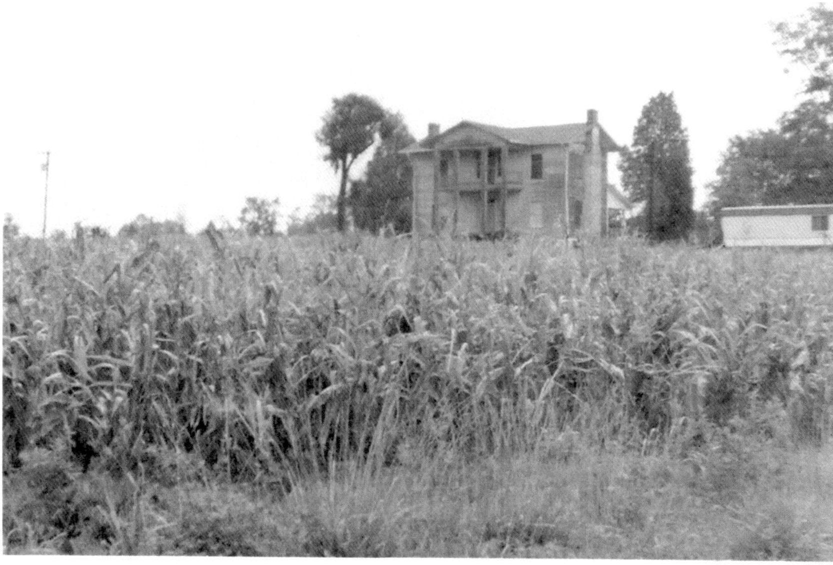

More recent photograph of the Dalton-Hunt house. *Photography by Frances H. Casstevens.*

been passed down to later generations. It was rumored that both Daisy and Will shared the same father—Dr. L.G. Hunt. If this was true, then Daisy and Will were half-brother and sister and their union was incestuous.

This might explain why Mrs. Hunt did not force Will Kelly to marry Daisy. Undoubtedly, Mrs. Hunt probably knew her daughter was pregnant. By February, Daisy was probably seven months into the pregnancy and her condition would have been hard to hide. In most situations, marriage would have been the most logical solution to the problem, but this situation was more complex. If Mrs. Hunt knew of Kelly's parentage, no wonder she was so opposed to the love affair. After she intercepted the note, perhaps she feared the couple was going to elope. She could not allow that to happen. There was only one solution and that was to kill Will Kelly. She may have done the deed herself.

The Life of Jack Hunt

The little fatherless boy had a miserable childhood. Because of his skin condition, he was kept hidden. Mrs. Lou Foster described Jack as being "good natured" and that he "loved people," but was deprived of the companionship of other neighborhood children and not even allowed to attend school. His grandmother did instill into him the "best manners of any boy I've seen," said

Mrs. Foster. But because of his isolation and coupled with his skin condition and illegitimate birth, Jack's personality was warped.

Jack was convicted of several serious crimes. He served a jail sentence for setting fire to the home of a neighbor, Frank Sofley. He was known to have killed at least two men. Jack ended his final days living in a small shack on the banks of the river, not far from his former home. He died December 2, 1972, at the age of seventy.

My father, Attorney F.D.B. Harding, once took me to Winston-Salem where he was to attend court. As we walked eastward on Fourth Street, we met a strange-looking man. My papa stopped to talk to the man for a moment. Afterward, I asked who that man was and my father replied, "That's Jack Hunt." As a child I had no idea who the man was or his tragic background.

Daisy Hunt and her son Jack continued to live with Mrs. Molly Hunt. Daisy died in 1934, and her mother died the next year. Ironically, the murder victim, Will Kelly, is buried directly behind Mrs. Hunt in the Huntsville Baptist Church cemetery.

For many years, the beautiful yet decaying mansion attracted curious young people in search of the ghosts that reportedly haunt it. The owner has surrounded the property by a sturdy fence, and the house is not open to the public. However, the haunting majesty of the place can still be seen from the road. It evokes visions of a way of life that flourished brightly for a time, then disappeared forever. See the appendix for the author's poem about the murder.

A Crime of Passion: The Murder of Ellen Smith

Poor Ellen Smith and How Was She Found,
Shot through the Heart
Lying Cold on the Ground.

One of the most famous murders occurred in the fashionable West End district of Winston-Salem, North Carolina. Residents were shocked when the body of a young girl, Ellen Smith, was found shot to death near the new Zinzendorf Hotel on West Fourth Street. The crime occurred on July 20, 1892.

Who Was Ellen Smith?

An engraving of Ellen Smith was published in the *Winston-Salem Sentinel* around the time the crime was committed. Subsequently, this picture was included in an article entitled "'Hear My Dying Words,' Sensational Murder Case Ended 85 Years Ago" by Alan Willis in the February 8, 1979 issue of the paper. Miss Smith is depicted as very attractive, with pleasant features and a good figure. An acquaintance described her as "not bad looking," although she had a "rather bold countenance" with a "rather sharp nose. Her short dark hair tended to curl and she had blue eyes and straight white teeth." Ellen probably had a dark complexion.

She may have moved to Winston to find employment. She may have worked as a maid at the new Zinzendorf Hotel. That she wore an apron when she was killed would indicate that she was a working girl.

Descendants of the Smith family of Yadkin County believe they are related to the murdered girl, as does local historian Lewis Brumfield. It is widely believed that Miss Ellen Smith was probably born in Yadkin County. The 1880 Yadkin County census lists Ellen Smith, age six, a mulatto, as the daughter of Julius Smith, white, and his wife, Julia, also listed as a mulatto. The family lived in the Baltimore section of the county.

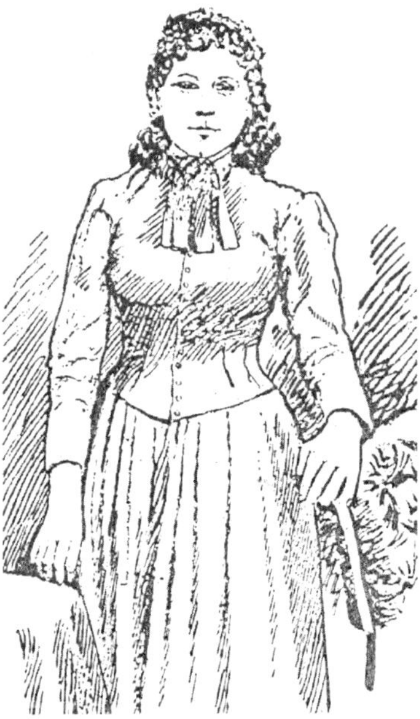

Ellen Smith, DeGraff's victim. *The Winston-Salem Sentinel, 1894.*

Julius Smith was the son of Thomas and Margaret Smith. In 1860 Julius H. Smith lived with his parents next door to Isaac Jarratt, a wealthy plantation owner who lived near the present Forbush Elementary School on Old Highway 421.

Julius Smith married Julia Head, daughter of Patsy Head, on August 5, 1873. Patsy Head was born in 1822 and died January 22, 1892. She is buried at the East Bend Baptist Church Cemetery. In 1880 Mary Head, age fifty-three, listed as "white," was living in the Smith household and was listed as "mother-in-law." If she was the mother of Julia Head, she is usually called "Patsy."

Many of the Smiths are buried at Enon Baptist Church, Yadkin County: Julius H. (April 5, 1854–December 31, 1944); his wife, Julia Head Smith (May 17, 1855–February 17, 1911); and Julius Smith's parents, Thomas L. Smith (August 31, 1831–March 17, 1915) and Margaret E. Smith (September 20, 1832–October 24, 1912). There was a marriage bond listed in Yadkin County dated December 4, 1852, for Thomas Smith to Margaret Binkley.

The census taker may have been wrong to list Julia and the Smith children as mulattos. This was a catchall category for anyone who was a bit dark-skinned. There were many people in Yadkin County with Indian ancestry. Melungeons, of mixed ancestry, were listed sometimes as white, at other times as mulatto.

The location of the graves of Ellen Smith and her child is unknown. If she is buried with the Smiths at Enon Baptist Church, her grave is unmarked.

THE MURDERER: PETER DEGRAFF

A sketch of Peter DeGraff by John Beard depicted him as a cartoon character with a large nose and a strangely shaped head. He wore a moustache and his hair, parted in the middle, was slicked down. DeGraff was born in Elizabeth City, North Carolina, in 1870. He had moved to Winston with his parents when he was only six years old. As a young man he began "to lead a reckless life." He

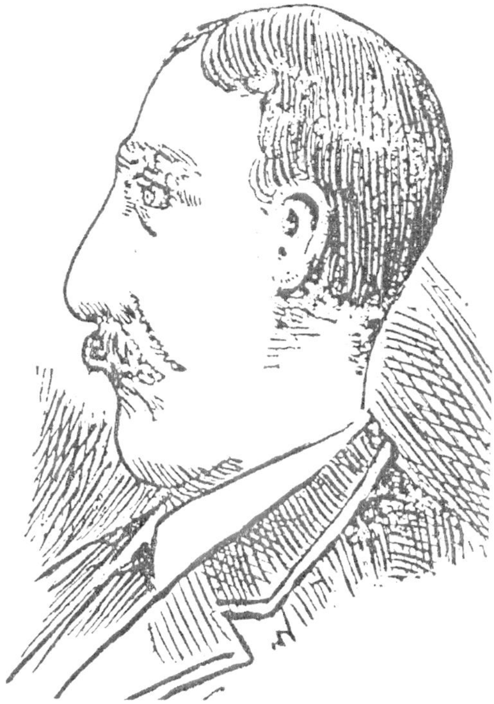

Peter DeGraff was hanged for the murder of his girlfriend. *The* Winston-Salem Sentinel*, 1894.*

started drinking whiskey and carrying a pistol. Once he was arrested for carrying a gun and was sentenced to jail, but he escaped and fled to Virginia. This was the first of a succession of run-ins with the law, escapes and flights from justice.

Little is known of Peter's family. Both his parents were alive at the time of his execution. He had a brother named Anthony, a basket maker, and a brother named Lee, a marble cutter, who lived on what is now Brookstown Avenue in Winston. Perhaps DeGraff was descended from Baron Christopher de Graffenreid, the founder of New Bern, North Carolina. The baron had purchased 17,500 acres on the Neuse and Trent Rivers. De Graffenreid arrived on September 10, 1710, with one hundred Swiss settlers and a town was surveyed and laid out. It was named New Bern, in honor of the Swiss city of the same name.

Events Preceding the Crime

While in his early twenties, Peter met seventeen-year-old Ellen Smith. They probably met while both were working at the new Zinzendorf Hotel in the West End of Winston. DeGraff was described in the newspapers as a "ladies' man" who had engaged in a number of affairs with young women. He had "ruined"

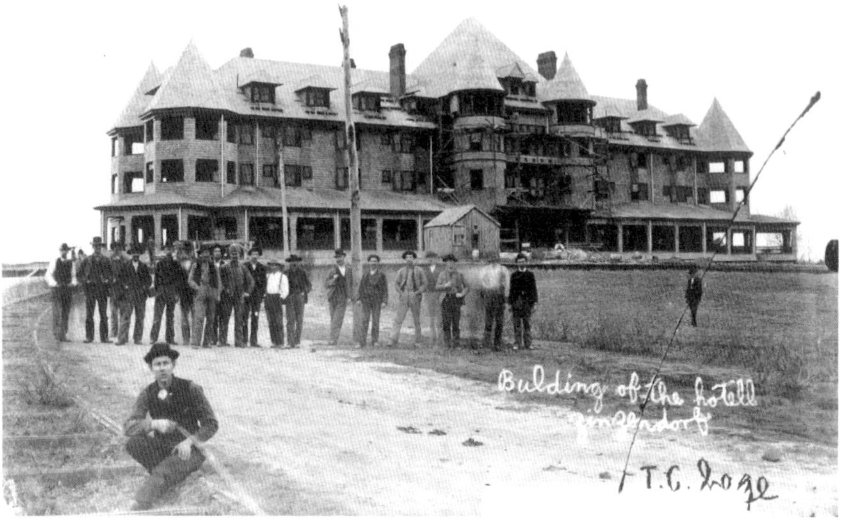

The first Zinzendorf Hotel where Ellen Smith worked. *Courtesy of the Forsyth County Public Library Photograph Collection.*

or "gotten in trouble" (gotten pregnant) many of those women. He would seduce a girl, then leave town to avoid matrimony; or he would initiate a quarrel to end the relationship. His relationship with Ellen apparently followed that pattern, and soon Ellen was in trouble. It was believed she had already borne DeGraff's child. That child reportedly died in infancy.

THE FACTS AND SCENE OF THE CRIME

Whether DeGraff initiated a quarrel to break off the relationship when Ellen began to push him to marry her or whether he was jealous of her relationship with another man is not known. Another theory is that Ellen wrote a note to Peter to tell him she did not want to see him any more. He replied and asked her to meet him in the woods behind the Zinzendorf (where her body was later found). A letter from him was found on her dead body, but the content is unknown.

According to a newspaper article written a few days after her body was found, Ellen had been "murdered in a thicket some distance from the west end of the car line, some time between Wednesday afternoon and Thursday morning. Her remains were found by a colored woman who says her discovery was made because a white man told her that a dead woman was in the bushes." Another witness testified that a man had told him there was a body lying in the thicket. If that man was DeGraff, he undoubtedly wanted the body of his lover to be found. Or could it have been someone else?

The murder took place behind the Zinzendorf Hotel near a spring in the woods at about 3:00 p.m. on July 20, 1892. Ellen's body was not discovered until the next morning at 8:00 a.m. The fatal bullet had passed through her body. The coroner ruled that she had been shot just once in the chest by a pistol held at close range. There were powder burns on her apron and dress.

The body of Ellen Smith was found in a patch of woods behind the hotel in the area where the YWCA tennis courts are today. Her killer had carefully placed her on a bed of greenery. Construction on the Zinzendorf West End Resort Hotel began in 1890 and was finished in 1892. This beautiful building at 1001West Fourth Street was designed by Wheelwright and Haven, architects, and was funded by the Sprague Electric Railway. It was part of a plan to develop the West End promoted by the West End Hotel and Land Company. The Zinzendorf was a rambling three-hundred-foot-long building on the crest of a hill. It had one hundred rooms, all heated by steam, and bathrooms on each floor. Guests could sit on the north veranda and look at the Sauratown Mountains. At night, they danced to the music of a twelve-piece orchestra.

The Hotel Zinzendorf, named for Count Nicholas Ludwig von Zinzendorf of Saxony, was noted for its eighteen-foot-wide porches. The grand hotel existed long enough to set a trend that led to hundreds of other houses being constructed with a "great welcoming porch." That trend is still evident in the homes that exist in the West End today.

The hotel attracted a few nationally known celebrities, such as General Adlai E. Stevenson I, the 1892 vice-presidential candidate. Thousands attended a parade in his honor as it passed through town.

In the 1890s the West End area of Winston-Salem, which included all of Fifth Street west of Poplar Street ("Millionaires Row"), had many fine houses. The Victorian-style home of R.J. Reynolds was in this area.

When streetcars were first established, one line ran west from the courthouse for one mile to the new Zinzendorf Hotel. Although the hotel was destroyed by fire on Thanksgiving Day in 1892, the streetcar track encouraged development in the West End. The fire at the hotel originated in the laundry room in the rear of the hotel about eleven o'clock in the morning. Firefighters from both Winston and Salem tried to put out the fire, but the water pressure was too low to be effective. The wooden building with cedar shingles was a pile of ashes in less than two hours.

Autopsy and Inquest

On July 21, 1892, coroner Augustus Fogle and a six-man jury heard testimony from the witnesses. An autopsy revealed that Miss Smith "came to her death by a pistol shot through the heart and that the deed was done by a companion, presumably the man who gave the first information." The man was supposedly Peter DeGraff, who had not been seen since the murder. A warrant, dated July 21, 1892, was issued for his arrest.

A newspaper article implied that DeGraff was the murdered girl's "paramour," and it reported that DeGraff had been "implicated in the Goins murder last year." Although a warrant had been issued for DeGraff, no bona fide effort was made to arrest him. Some thought the sheriff had been careless; others laid a charge of "cowardice" against the sheriff. There was also speculation that DeGraff had not yet been arrested because he had knowledge of "extraordinary settlement of other cases, than the Sheriff would like to have divulged." For this reason, DeGraff had been allowed to escape arrest. The reporter asked "why persons charged with murder are thus permitted to strut about the country in broad daylight, while our officers timidly keep out of their way." The reporter even went so far as to say that if DeGraff knew some dangerous secrets, then a public meeting should be called and the governor of the state asked to "order out troops to protect our people against murders and those who have compounded with them."

Was this just rumor and gossip? The above article certainly did not give a good character reference to DeGraff, but hinted that he had been involved in another murder and had information regarding other cases in which the sheriff had not made an arrest.

Reportedly, Peter bravely showed himself to many individuals and sent word to the sheriff to come and get him. The sheriff of Forsyth County failed to do so but as soon as he was replaced by a new sheriff, Peter DeGraff was promptly arrested.

Flight to Avoid Arrest

There are two conflicting stories about DeGraff's movements after the crime. One is that he remained in the area; the other is that he fled immediately.

A month after the murder, Peter DeGraff was still free. The *Salem People's Press* noted that DeGraff had been joined by four others who were also successful in "eluding arrest and yet whose whereabouts are well known." The case was beginning to draw attention from other cities. An article in the *Raleigh State Chronicle* charged Sheriff Teague of Forsyth County with negligence and stated in no uncertain terms that an "officer of the law in North Carolina is persistent in breaking the requirements of that law and is letting an accused murderer walk under his very nose unmolested with all impunity."

When things got too hot in Forsyth, Peter fled to the mountains. He later told the authorities that he even spent the night with the sheriff of Ashe County, during which time he and the sheriff discussed the "notorious Peter DeGraff case."

DeGraff Arrested

On June 23, 1893, Sheriff McArthur received a tip that DeGraff had been seen getting off the train at Rural Hall. Officers were dispatched to his parents' home and to places he was known to frequent, but Peter had returned to the scene of the crime. He was observed by witnesses as he cried out, "Ellen, if you are in heaven arise; if in hell, stay there."

Later that evening, DeGraff was found hiding under a feather "tick" (mattress) in a home near the tavern where he had once worked. The arrest was made by Sheriff McArthur and Officer J.J. Adams. When the officers demanded that DeGraff surrender, he replied, "All right, Mr. Adams, I'll give up. I want you to treat me like a gentleman though." The officers agreed not to harm him, as long as he behaved himself. Another account stated that DeGraff rode to the jail on a horse behind Officer Adams.

It was rumored that after the murder, DeGraff had fled to Mount Airy, about fifty miles away. He remained there for nearly a year. Thinking he was safe, DeGraff boarded a train and got off at Rural Hall. The Forsyth County sheriff received a tip that DeGraff had been seen in that area. The sheriff and his officers found him in the home of Gideon Russell on what is now Country Club Road.

Trial and Conviction

DeGraff was arrested and charged with murder in the first degree. The trial began on August 11, 1893, before Judge Robert W. Winston. Prosecutor for the State was Clement Manly. DeGraff was represented by Attorneys Colonel Thomas H. Sutton and Frank T. Baldwin. DeGraff took the stand but did not help his case. He said that he returned to the scene of the crime because he had heard an old saying that if a person who committed a murder went back to the crime scene and spoke the right words, the victim would appear. That one statement sealed DeGraff's fate because he had been observed doing that very thing. One of the jurors stated that DeGraff's testimony about why he had returned to the spring in the woods had given him away. DeGraff was either very stupid or he felt guilty for his crime and wanted to be caught and punished. Or perhaps he wanted to tell Ellen he was sorry.

The trial lasted only three days. The jury deliberated for twelve hours before returning with a verdict of guilty at 8:30 a.m. on the morning of August 15. The next day, Judge Winston sentenced DeGraff to death. DeGraff appealed to the North Carolina Supreme Court but was denied a new trial. His appeal was based on several technicalities, but the lower court verdict was upheld. Chief Justice Shepherd's opinion mentioned DeGraff's flight from justice to Roanoke, Virginia, and then to New Mexico.

The case was appealed to North Carolina Governor Julian S. Carr for a stay of execution, but the governor refused. The execution was set for Thursday, February 8, 1894.

While awaiting his execution, DeGraff spent his last days protesting his innocence. He wrote letters to the local papers and claimed to "forgive his persecutors." He predicted that after he was gone, the man who actually committed the crime would be discovered. DeGraff was not taken seriously and one newspaper suggested that he be examined to validate his sanity.

The night before he was to hang, Peter was visited by a group of young men who sang and prayed with him. They may be among those who tried to get DeGraff to confess his guilt. He did not, and after everyone left, DeGraff slept peacefully with the help of "sleeping powders." The next morning, he arose, ate breakfast and dressed in the new black suit the county had provided for the occasion. The prisoner said his farewells to his family and he begged his father not to attend the hanging because of his age and ill health.

EXECUTION

Peter DeGraff was escorted from the jail to the place of execution by J.E. Ziglar, the jailer, Sheriff McArthur, Mayor E.E. Gray and an unnamed reporter for the *Sentinel*. Crowds lined the streets all along the route. They rode out Liberty Street in a closed carriage to the place of execution at the county poorhouse. This was across from where the Z. Smith Reynolds airport is now. A grave had already been dug in "potter's field." According to some, the execution was held at the old fair grounds in Winston.

At the time of his execution, DeGraff was twenty-four years old. People came from miles around to see the gruesome event. Some accounts estimate the crowd as high as six thousand. The scene had a carnival atmosphere.

S.S. Kinney, who was ninety-five in 1975, attended the execution when he was only fourteen years old. Kinney walked from his home on Belews Creek

Road to the place where the execution was to be held. It was a rather cold day. Kinney recalled that an area had been roped off around the scaffold to keep the spectators from getting too close. He managed to get in a position about thirty feet from the gallows. He saw Peter DeGraff arrive accompanied by several men, and he noted that DeGraff "appeared undisturbed as he mounted the scaffold." The Reverend H.A. Brown, pastor of the First Baptist Church, offered a prayer for DeGraff's parents and family, and he prayed that God would allow DeGraff to make a statement before he was hanged.

Advice from the Gallows

As Peter DeGraff climbed up to the scaffold, he took off his hat. After the rope was placed around his neck, he bowed to the crowd. As the death sentence was being read, the man who had been convicted of murder showed no sign of nervousness. He then asked to make a statement. The crowd was eager to hear what he had to say because from the time he was arrested, all during his trial and his subsequent imprisonment, DeGraff had maintained he was innocent of the murder. S.S. Kinney recalled the "crowd gasping" when Peter declared, "I killed Ellen Smith."

Frank Whitaker of the Center community in Yadkin County recalled that Peter said that he loved Ellen and intended to marry her. Whitaker recalled that the condemned man warned all "against liquor and bad women." He claimed that he was drunk when he killed the nineteen-year-old Ellen. That was his only excuse for the murder of his sweetheart. After he finished speaking, the sheriff kicked the block from under DeGraff's feet and he dropped to his death.

Regardless of where the hanging took place, DeGraff confessed and his last words were a warning: "I stand here today to receive my just reward. I again say to the people here, beware of bad women and whiskey…don't put your hands on cards, bad women and dice. Hear my dying words."

Immortalized in Song

After DeGraff's execution, public sentiment was both for and against him. Reportedly, while in prison, DeGraff wrote the first version of the song that became so popular with the public that it was declared a misdemeanor to sing in a gathering of any size because it was sure to start a riot.

One early version, entitled "Ellen Smith," by Tom Sauber, was set to the tune of "How Firm a Foundation." The story of DeGraff's killing his girlfriend has been recorded by various groups, including the Country Gentlemen, whose version begins, "Poor Ellen Smith how was she found / Shot through the heart lying cold on the ground." Their version does not stick to the facts, and one verse has DeGraff being held in prison for twenty years. (See appendix for words.)

The tragic story of "Poor Ellen Smith" has been recorded by many artists in the bluegrass music field, including Frank Profitt, the Stanley Brothers, Doc and Merle Watson, Wilma Lee and Stoney Cooper, Jimmy Martin, Don Reno, Kingston Trio, Lester Flat and Earl Scruggs, New Lost City Ramblers, Kossoy Sisters, George Pegram and Tommy Jarrell.

This tragic love story will undoubtedly continue to live on in the folk music and folklore of America.

Recent Information

In the 1970s, the Forsyth County sheriff's department moved into new offices in the Hall of Justice. In searching for pictures of former sheriffs, Mr. John H. Winder donated a picture of Sheriff R.M. McArthur, Winder's grandfather. Mr. Winder also donated a number of old documents. Among them was the order for the execution of Peter DeGraff. It had been sent to Sheriff McArthur by Governor Elias Carr on January 2, 1894. The order decreed that Peter DeGraff was to be hanged "by the neck until he is dead." The order further directed the sheriff to carry out the hanging "at the usual place," as prescribed by county law. Some sources say the hanging occurred in the present Hanes Park near Wiley School. Other sources insist that DeGraff was hanged on a tree near the end of North Trade Street. All agree that the hanging attracted a large crowd of onlookers. One contemporary source placed the execution site "near the Snipes slaughter House, just beyond the incorporate limits of East Winston." Based on an 1894 article in the *Yadkin Valley News*, Surry County historian Ruth Minick wrote that the hanging was carried out on a scaffold that had been set up "near the county home, four miles this side of Winston." That would be on the north side toward Mount Airy.

Unidentified Skeleton in the Woods

He wore a white gold ring on his right hand, with initials T.H.P. engraved.

On Sunday, July 30, 1939, the badly decomposed body of a man was found in some woods east of Yadkinville, about twenty-five yards from Old Highway 421. The site was between the old Phillips home place and the creek.

A path led from the highway down the hill to a shaded place known to be frequented by men who enjoyed a game of poker now and then. The body was found by Buck Nicks and Exie Harding, who were walking through the woods near the highway. The two men had gone into the woods to hide a pint of liquor.

At the time the remains were found, the skull and feet lay some distance away from the body. The skull had been pierced by a bullet that appeared to have entered from the right side and exited on the opposite side. A .32-caliber automatic Colt revolver lay on the ground near the body. A crew of men using a shovel, rake and sieve found a cartridge, which had been shot from an automatic pistol near where the pistol was found.

Jonah Williams was in the habit of passing by the area where the body was found every morning. He told the police that he began smelling a foul odor about two months before the remains were actually discovered. A copy of the April issue of *The Ladies Home Journal* was found lying under the remains of the body, which placed the death sometime between April and July. A poker card, the king of diamonds, was found at the scene.

Bill Rutledge and Trig Howell, directed by Attorney Boone Harding, found the man's lower dentures and a man's handkerchief embroidered in one corner with the letter M. They also found some straight and slightly gray hair, which indicated he was an older white male.

Word quickly spread of the discovery of the corpse, and it was estimated that some five thousand people came to view the murder scene. Several people came to look at the articles found with the body in hopes of identifying a missing relative. The unidentified body was placed in a box and buried in the county home cemetery.

THE MOTIVE

No billfold or any money was found on the body. Perhaps the victim had been caught cheating at cards—a frequent cause for anger and violence—or the motive may have been robbery. Suicide is another possibility. If the man had lost at cards, the cause of death may have been suicide, since the bullet entered from the right side of the head. The gun was found on the right side of the body with the safety off.

CLUES TO THE IDENTITY

The available evidence was scant. The man wore an expensive blue suit and a vest. A gray felt hat was found and a pair of size eight shoes, which was small for a man. He wore long, heavy underwear, an indication that it was still cool weather when he died. He had on a neatly tied necktie in a solid dark color and a white shirt. Two front teeth of his upper dentures had gold crowns, an expensive bit of dental work. He wore a double truss of metal (for a double hernia). These clues could probably have led to his identity with today's modern forensic technology and communications capabilities.

In the dead man's pockets were found some unusual items: four lead pencils, one fountain pen, a pack of small rubber bands, a pair of scissors (four inches long), a pocket knife, a pipe and smoking tobacco pouch and two small black combs. There was a nice watch chain (but the watch was missing), several pieces of shoestring, a pair of glasses and a case. The combs were in the glasses case instead of the glasses.

One possible clue to the man's identity was found inside the white gold ring he wore on his right hand, on which the initials T.H.P. were engraved. It appeared to be an expensive ring but it had a cheap red setting. Yet even with this clue, no one came forward to identify and claim the body.

After weeks of investigation, Guy Scott of the State Bureau of Investigation and his staff came to the conclusion that the dead man was of Scotch-Irish descent and was between fifty-five and sixty years old. They discovered that he wore a moustache because remains of it were found. He wore glasses, smoked a pipe and carried his tobacco in a pouch.

It was suggested that perhaps the body was that of John Doyle, who had been missing "from his shack in Greensboro since May 20." Doyle had been the object of an extensive search but had not been found. Bob Hauser, who knew Doyle, came to Yadkinville and examined the articles found with the man in the woods. Hauser did not believe that the unidentified may was Doyle. However, he told authorities that Doyle was known to have "had much money on his person."

Several people came from High Point to examine the dead man's effects in hopes of finding a missing relative without success.

The state of forensic medicine at that time was not advanced enough to enable authorities to identify the dead man or who had killed him.

Was The Victim McDougall?

The *Herald,* another Yadkinville paper, proclaimed the body was that of Wallace McDougall, an engraver and cartoonist. Wallace traveled the country working for various newspapers. McDougall had worked for a newspaper in Yadkinville, but he had been gone for some months.

That theory was quickly discarded in 1941 when Wallace McDougall stepped off the bus in Yadkinville on his way from Florida to Winston-Salem. Since leaving Yadkinville in 1939, McDougall had been traveling the country. He had worked for the *Chicago Herald-Examiner* for a while and then moved to St. Paul. He had also been employed to draw cartoons for the Wendell Wilkie presidential campaign. McDougall was shocked to learn he was believed to have been the badly decomposed body found in the woods. The dead man was definitely not Wallace McDougall, as reported previously and erroneously by the *Renfro Herald.*

It is easy to understand why some thought the body was that of Wallace McDougall. There were several similarities between McDougall and the dead man. Both were between fifty-five and sixty years old. The items in the dead man's pocket could have belonged to a draftsman or an artist. McDougall's name started with an M, which was the initial on the handkerchief found at the scene. McDougall had worked for the *Herald,* and two people had identified the clothing found on the dead man as belonging to McDougall. However, McDougall always smoked a corncob pipe, instead of the kind of pipe found at the scene of the crime. McDougall was also a Scotch-Irishman who had come to Yadkinville seeking employment. He also had worked for some time with a Mocksville newspaper before leaving the area.

The same questions remain in 2006 that were asked in 1939: Who was the man? Where was the watch that was missing from the expensive chain? Had he been murdered and robbed or had he committed suicide?

The skeleton in the woods was never identified. Although cause of death was listed as a gunshot wound to the head, it was undetermined whether it was murder or suicide.

Two Yadkinville residents said they had always heard that the murder was committed by a well-known Yadkinville businessman. This man, now deceased, was known to have a hot temper and to have become embroiled in several altercations. Without more substantial evidence and indisputable proof, the man's identity cannot be revealed. The case of the skeleton in the woods remains one of Yadkin County's unsolved mysteries.

Domestic Violence Can Be Fatal

Jesus says it's time to go.

Some places on Earth are sacred; others are evil. Certain places seem to attract violence and harbor unexplained events. The plantation that once belonged to Samuel Speer is one such place. In this quiet, rural setting of Yadkin County, violence has erupted more than once, about four miles east of Yadkinville on Old Highway 421.

Early pioneers, including Samuel's father, Henry Speer, came to North Carolina from Maryland about 1770. Henry served as a captain in the American Revolution. He was elected a representative from Surry County to the North Carolina General Assembly. He was also a county commissioner and a town commissioner for Rockford in Surry County. As a surveyor, Henry Speer surveyed land for others and the adjoining land for himself. He surveyed the road from Rockford to the Shallow Ford (Huntsville) and was awarded the contract to build a bridge over Deep Creek. The road that crosses that bridge has been called "Speer Bridge Road" ever since that time, in honor of Henry Speer.

Sometime after 1800, Henry took his wife and family and moved to Kentucky. Henry kept on going, surveying and buying land as he went. Henry is believed to have died in Indiana, but his place of burial is unknown.

His son Samuel returned and settled in Surry (now Yadkin County), where, in 1812, he married a widow, Ruth "Cain" Eddleman. Samuel and his family lived in a fine two-story "folk-Federal-style house" with a large basement, as described in 1985 by architectural historian Kirk Mohney. The logs of the house were later covered with weatherboards. Eventually, the roof was lowered and the house converted to a one-story pack house and storage building. In 1835 Samuel Speer listed 8 tracts of land totaling 987.5 acres valued at $2,691, located in Surry (now Yadkin) County. When Yadkin County was formed from Surry in 1850, Samuel was appointed county surveyor.

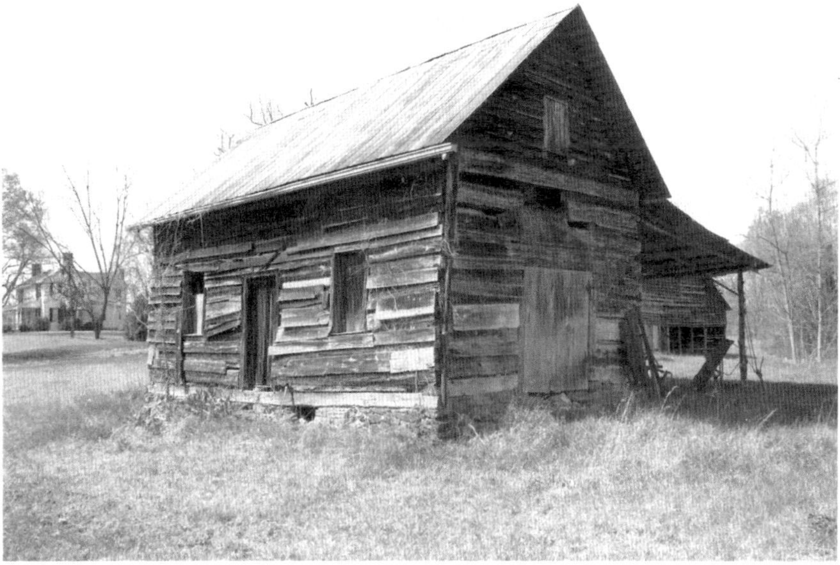

The old Samuel Speer house near Yadkinville was recently demolished. *Courtesy of the Yadkin County Historical Society.*

Samuel's wife died in 1847, and she was buried in the Speer-Harding cemetery near the Speer home. Beside her lies the couple's first son, Squire Madison Speer, who died in 1822.

A year after his wife's death, Samuel, age sixty-nine, married a younger woman named Nancy. It was not a happy marriage.

Illicit Sex and Scandal

In 1855, after only seven years of marriage, Samuel's second wife, Nancy, filed for a divorce. She claimed that he was having adulterous affairs with several women. This was at a time when divorce was extremely rare and was detrimental to the reputation of the parties involved. According to Nancy's petition, she and Samuel lived in "peace and happiness" for the first year of their marriage. She alleged that Speer began visiting the house of Caroline Dinkins and that Caroline visited Speer in his home. When Nancy confronted her husband and begged him to cease his activities with "this bad woman," he "flew into a violent rage, drew a knife and compelled her to flee for safety with one of the neighbors." Nancy also claimed that in April of 1851, while she was lying sick in bed, Samuel held a "large stick over her head and threatened her life if she did not immediately leave his house." She was so afraid of him that she went to the house of her sister

Elizabeth Mitchel and remained for four months. Nancy also stated that Caroline Dinkins had delivered a child fathered by Samuel Speer.

In 1855, the year his wife filed for divorce, Samuel was seventy-seven years old. If his wife's allegations were true, Sam Speer must have been quite remarkable. It is known that he had at least one illegitimate child whose date of birth was written in his family Bible. In order to let things cool down, Samuel pulled up stakes and moved with his daughter, Jane; her husband, William Harding; and their children to Texas in the fall of 1855. His daughter did not like Texas and the group returned to Yadkin County the next year.

By 1860 Samuel Speer and his second wife were living in separate households. Nancy Speer, age forty, was listed in Forbush Township. Samuel Speer Sr., age eighty-two, surveyor, was listed as living in Yadkinville with Caroline Jarvis Dinkins, age forty-five.

Samuel Speer died on December 26, 1868. His home and 475 acres were bought by Thomas Davis in 1876. Thomas Davis then sold the property to his sons, John and Eli Thomas Davis. Eli Thomas took the eastern half and John Davis took the western half.

In 1882 John Henry Davis (1850–1920) built a large two-story farmhouse only a few yards from the old Samuel Speer house. Although nothing tragic is known to have occurred in the John Henry Davis house, some of those who lived in the house in the last quarter of the twentieth century told stories of seeing the ghost of a little old lady.

The John Henry Davis property, including the old Samuel Speer house, was recently purchased by a developer, who demolished the ancient Speer house.

Tragedies Caused by Fire

Eli Thomas Davis was prominent in the community. He was a farmer, merchant, educator and devoted family man. Eli Thomas built a large two-story hipped-roof house in 1882 and remodeled it about 1890.

Eli's home was inherited by his son, Paul Price Davis. However, on Easter Sunday morning in April of 1948, a man returning from the Moravian Easter services in Salem saw smoke coming from the house. He stopped and took a number of photographs of the structure being consumed by flames. The house was rebuilt in 1950, and it became a showplace as the home of Paul Price Davis. This stately white-columned Southern colonial house was surrounded by immaculate landscaped grounds. Davis could afford a beautiful house because he owned Davis Department Store in Winston-Salem.

The only son of Paul Price Davis, Charles Bruce Davis, died at age thirty-nine on December 23, 1973, in a mysterious fire in one of the outbuildings on the property. The fire may have been caused by a cigarette. Bruce eventually died from burns and smoke inhalation when the cot on which he was sleeping caught fire. According to the local paper, Bruce had been "receiving medical treatment for about two weeks for chest congestion." On the day of his death, he had been rounding up some cows that had gotten outside the fence. He went into a storage building to feed a dog confined there. A short time later, his body was discovered by his fourteen-year-old son who saw smoke coming from the building. An autopsy revealed that the deceased had hardening of the arteries and may have had a coronary artery attack. Carbon monoxide poisoning from burning oil on the floor and a burning mattress was stated as the cause of death.

Father Goes Berserk

About two hundred yards east of the old Samuel Speer house and the family graveyard once stood a small white-frame house. This insignificant little structure had a tragic history. An event occurred there in 1947 that was reminiscent of the famous Lawson family murders in Stokes County.

The rent house was owned by Paul Price Davis, who maintained a large farm. A number of tenants had occupied the little house at one time or another. One of the tenants was Eugene "Gene" Scales, age thirty-one; his wife, Ruth Porter Scales, age twenty; and their three children: Dorothy Ann, age eight; Grace Helen, age six; and Alice Fay, age two.

On the night of January 30, 1947, Scales suddenly declared, "Jesus says it's time to go!" before grabbing his three girls and throwing them into a well on the back porch of the house. He tried to push his wife into the well, but failed. He then jumped into the well himself, and landed on the children who lay in four feet of water at the bottom of the well. After a few moments, Mrs. Scales called to her husband and asked if he was hurt and if he could climb back out. He replied, "When the Lord tells me to come back up, I'll come." After several minutes of thrashing around he shouted that he was coming up. She lowered the well bucket to help him, but the windlass broke under his weight. Finally, he managed to climb to the top of the narrow well.

Mrs. Scales then ran to a neighbor's house and called Sheriff Bill Moxley. After the officers arrived, the bodies of the children were removed from the well. The new coroner, Jake F. Brown, ruled that an inquest was unnecessary. A postmortem examination confirmed the fact that the children had died from drowning.

Scales was arrested and taken into custody. He told Sheriff Moxley, "I must have gone crazy." Scales was from Tobaccoville and was held in high esteem by his employer, Mr. Paul Price Davis. He was to be tried the following week when the superior court convened in Yadkinville.

The February term of the superior court opened on Monday, February 3, with Judge H. Hoyle Sink of Greensboro presiding. Attorney Avalon E. Hall was the prosecutor. Scales was charged with first-degree murder but his attorney, J. Earle McMichael, told the court that Scales was unable to testify because he was insane. The court then ordered a sanity hearing. Four witnesses were called to testify, and the jury reached its verdict in only five minutes that the defendant was "of unsound mind." Judge Sink then ordered the defendant to be confined in the state hospital at Goldsboro.

DEATH STRIKES AGAIN IN THE RENT HOUSE

Fourteen years later in the summer of 1961, a middle-aged couple and their two children occupied the same little tenant house on the Davis property. James A. Williams liked to drink the illegal brew called moonshine or white lightning. Generally a mild-mannered and quiet person, when intoxicated, Williams could become abusive.

It was early in the morning, and he had been drinking all night. His wife, Betty, pleaded with him to put away the liquor and they argued. "Shut up," he shouted at his wife, and he picked up his double-barreled shotgun and pulled the trigger. Pellets from the twelve-gauge shotgun struck her in the wrist and chest. The children heard the shot and came running into the room to find their mother lying on the floor. He spoke to the children and told them, "I'm going to do the same thing to myself," and he picked up the gun and some shells and left the house. He did not forget his jar of liquor.

An ambulance was called and with it came the sheriff, who had asked to borrow bloodhounds from Sparta. When the dogs arrived, a search of the woods north of the house was made. Within a short time, the dogs had tracked the man and found him sitting with his gun and his jar of liquor. As the officers approached, the man shot himself in the left shoulder. (It is not easy to commit suicide with a rifle or shotgun because of the length of the barrel.)

Williams was taken to the hospital. In less than two weeks, he was on trial for the murder of his wife. Only ten days and two hours after he had shot and killed his wife, Williams plead guilty to the crime and was automatically sentenced to life in prison. The little house, which was the site of so much tragedy, has been demolished.

Murder or Suicide: The Mysterious Death of Z. Smith Reynolds

Moanin' Low

Zachary Smith Reynolds had everything anyone could possibly want—fame, fortune, a beautiful wife and a mansion—or so it seemed. Yet before he was twenty-one years old, Smith Reynolds was found dead from a gunshot wound to the head. The death of Zachary Smith Reynolds was one of the top stories of 1932, ranking third behind the Lindberg baby kidnapping and the election of Franklin D. Roosevelt as president of the United States. The investigation into the death of Z. Smith Reynolds was badly handled and, even after seventy-four years, the case remains unsolved. Was Reynolds's untimely death murder or suicide?

Reynolds was born in Winston-Salem, North Carolina, in 1911 to Richard Joshua and Katherine Smith Reynolds. He was the youngest of four children. Smith, as he was called, was only seven when his father died and a teenager when his mother died. He was brought up by his uncle, Will Reynolds, and aunt, Kate Bitting Reynolds. (Will Reynolds's property, now owned by Forsyth County, is known as Tanglewood Park.)

Smith, a handsome young man with a cleft chin, had an innocent boyish-looking face. He was enrolled in the finest college-preparatory schools, but he quit school to devote his time to flying. He was very interested in the growing field of aviation (Smith Reynolds Airport is named after him) and he soon became an accomplished pilot. In 1932 he flew solo from London to Hong Kong. The young pilot proved he could be disciplined, cool-headed and capable of making difficult decisions while in the air on long flights.

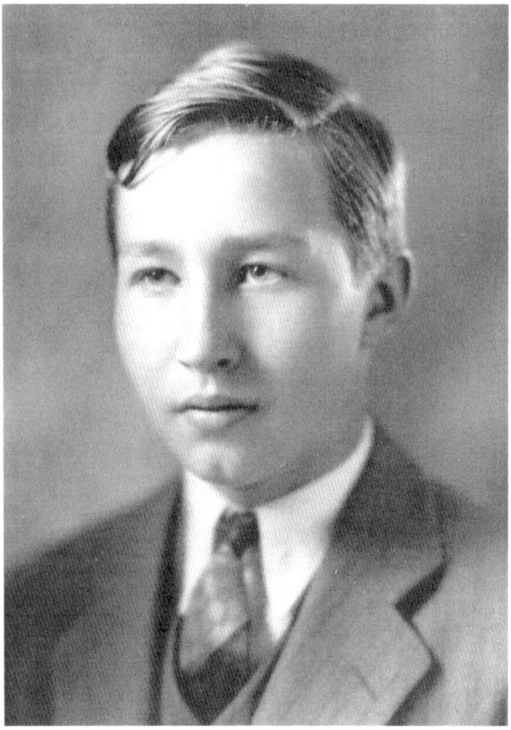

Z. Smith Reynolds. *Courtesy of Reynolda House Museum of American Art.*

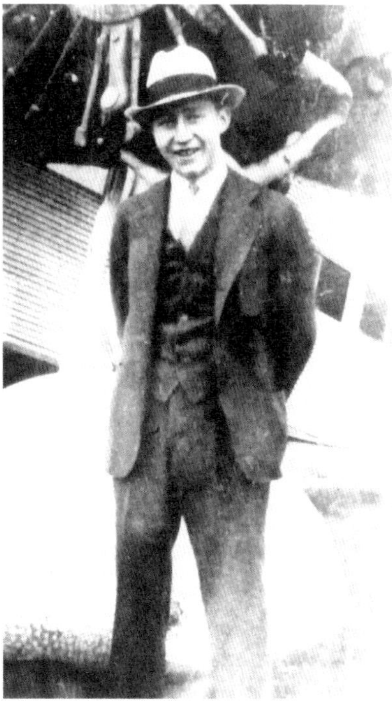

Z. Smith Reynolds with his tri-motor airplane. *Courtesy of Reynolda House Museum of American Art.*

Smith's First Marriage

On the ground, the experienced pilot sometimes acted immature and impulsive. When he was only eighteen, he married Anne Cannon, the daughter of the Cannon towel baron, Joseph F. Cannon. It was a shotgun wedding—Anne's father had caught the two of them in bed together. Smith and Anne were married quickly in York, South Carolina, on November 16, 1929. Mr. Cannon was wise to force the marriage, since in less than nine months, Anne gave birth to a baby girl. Shortly after the birth of the child, Smith flew Anne to Reno to obtain a divorce. Smith reportedly said, "She liked big parties, and I like little parties." Anne received a large sum of money when the divorce became final.

Smith Meets Libby

Although barely eighteen when Zachary Smith Reynolds met Libby Holman, he was smitten. He asked her to marry him even before his divorce from Anne Cannon was final. He was infatuated with the singer and swore he would kill himself if she did not marry him. Reluctantly, Libby finally accepted and the couple was married November 29, 1931, by a justice of the peace in Monroe, Michigan. They kept their marriage a secret for a while but eventually the truth came out.

Smith Reynolds probably met Libby Holman when he visited his brother, R.J. "Dick" Reynolds Jr., in New York. The brothers had a riotous time and enjoyed all the entertainment offered by the big city. Dick introduced Smith to Libby in Baltimore where she was acting in *Three's A Crowd.* Smith and Libby had a few dates, usually after she had finished play rehearsals and performances.

Libby was way out of his league. Seven years older than Smith physically, Libby was years ahead emotionally and in worldly experience. Yet Reynolds was accustomed to getting what he wanted, and he wanted Libby. However, when he married her, Smith got more than he could handle. The marriage to the twenty-five-year-old "torch singer" took place only six days after his divorce from Anne Cannon.

Libby Holman (real name Elsbeth Holzman) was born on May 23, 1904, in Cincinnati, Ohio. Her family was of German-Jewish origins on both sides. Libby was well educated and intelligent, and her attorney father encouraged her to attend law school after she graduated from college.

After graduating from college, Libby went to New York to enter law school, but when she got a part in Channing Pollack's play *The Fool*, she knew that she belonged on the stage. Although *The Fool* folded on tour, Libby was on her way to stardom.

The olive-skinned, coal-black-haired Libby was unusual-looking. Leonard Sillman, a friend and adviser of Libby's, described her as having "slits for eyes, and a bee-stung mouth, and a somewhat unreliable singing voice." Lucinda

Ballard, a costume designer, described Libby as having a "certain quality which doesn't show up in photos. Her skin had extraordinary texture and while her hair often looked messy, it had a beautiful sheen." One of her most remarkable features was her eyes, which were "a changeable greenish-hazel color," and which stood out in marked contrast to her "tawny complexion."

With her throaty voice, Libby became famous for singing "Moanin' Low" in *The Little Show,* which opened in 1929. Her costars were Clifton Webb and Fred Allen. The musical opened on Broadway and received great reviews from critics and the public. After that, Libby was hailed as the "premier torch singer" on Broadway. She appeared in a number of Broadway musicals: *Merry-Go-Round*, *Garric Gaieties*, *Rainbow* and *Three's A Crowd.*

In the last years of the Roaring Twenties, Libby and her friends lived wild and high. They frequented nightclubs and speakeasies. They drank and experimented with all kinds of illegal and legal drugs. With her friends Tallulah Bankhead and Jeanne Eagles, she made the rounds of the clubs in Harlem in search of cocaine, opium or marijuana. With her salary of $2,000 a week for performing in *The Little Show*, Libby could afford anything.

Libby seemed to prefer women, but she had affairs with men as well. Her closest friends were either bisexual (such as Tallulah Bankhead, Jeanne Eagles and Louisa Carpenter Du Point Jenney) or homosexual (such as Clifton Webb and Montgomery Clift).

When Libby met Jeanne Eagles, they were instantly attracted to each other. Jeanne seemed to be very happy with their relationship and she moved in with Libby. The pair was seen everywhere together—playing tennis, drinking, singing, dancing. When Eagles died at age thirty-nine of an overdose of chloral hydrate ("knockout drops") and heroin, Libby was devastated.

MARRIED LIFE

During the summer of 1932, Smith convinced Libby to come to Reynolda, his home in Winston-Salem, North Carolina. Reynolda House was always filled with guests eager to partake of the abundant supply of alcoholic beverages, the pool and a variety of entertainments.

The idea for Reynolda House was conceived by Smith's mother, Mrs. Katherine Smith Reynolds. Early in life, Katherine, of Mount Airy, North Carolina, knew what she wanted. She confided to her college roommate in 1899: "When I marry, I shall go to Europe on my wedding trip, and I shall bring home a wonderful work of art. And then I shall buy a great estate and I shall have a thousand cattle on a hill and flowers all around." Her wish came true when in

1904 Katherine married Richard Joshua Reynolds, founder of R.J. Reynolds Tobacco Company.

Katherine's wealthy husband built Reynolda House in the center of a thousand-acre tract of land Mrs. Reynolds had acquired on the outskirts of Winston-Salem. R.J. Reynolds died in 1918, a year after the house was completed. Mrs. Reynolds died in 1924.

The Night of July 4

On Sunday afternoon, July 4, 1932, Libby and her guest and friend from New York, Blanche Yurka, were reading a play Blanche was interested in seeing produced. Smith sat and listened for a while but soon became bored. An incident occurred that angered Smith, although the retelling of the incident was contradictory. One version is that Smith, sitting at the foot of Libby's chaise lounge, put his arm on her bare thigh. She brushed it aside. Smith sat there a few more minutes, then got up and left. Albert "Ab" Walker, a young man who was a friend and also an employee, testified at the inquest that Libby Reynolds had told him she placed her hand on Smith's leg but he moved it away. Later, she denied doing that to her husband. He replied, "You either did or I am insane; I will go down and see a physician." No matter who did what, Smith and Ab went to town and spent that night in the Robert E. Lee Hotel, where the two young men got drunk. It was also reported that they were entertained by a couple of prostitutes from Norfolk, Virginia. Smith and Ab returned to Reynolda about 7:00 a.m., before anyone else was up. In his testimony at the inquest, Ab stated that Smith had confided to him that he "might be insane." Was Libby deliberately trying to make Smith think he was losing his mind, or was it she who was confused from drinking and taking drugs?

Charlie Hill's twenty-first birthday was a good excuse for a party, which could also serve as a send-off party for Smith before he began his pending flight around the world. Some of the guests were Mrs. William Vaught, the former Mary Louise Collier; Charles Norfleet, son of the head of the trust department at Wachovia Bank & Trust Company; and Jim Shepherd. There was also Lewin McGinnis, who ran the local airport and coached Smith in flying, and Blanche Yurka. Raymond Kramer, a tutor, was staying at Reynolda but he had not been invited to the party.

The Fatal Night

The party on the night of July 5, 1932, was not much different from many other gatherings, except that when this party ended, Zachary Smith Reynolds was dead. By midnight, all of the guests had left Reynolda except those who were staying overnight. Mrs. William Vaught retired early after her drive with Jim Shepard, as did Blanche Yurka. Smith and Ab remained up. Ab had known Smith practically all his life. Ab's father was wealthy, but most of his cash was tied up in real estate. Ab, an unimpressive young man, was unemployed at the time Smith returned to Winston-Salem, and he welcomed the chance to work as a "secretary" for Reynolds.

The sequence of events that night is vague. Libby had drunk too much at the party, and Smith was not pleased by the way she flirted with the guests. It was plain, even to the staff, that Smith was not enjoying the party. He had not wanted the party in the first place. Although those who were at the party later stated that there was little drinking, this was probably an understatement if not an outright lie.

Smith noticed Ab following Libby wherever she went. When the party began to break up, Smith was the first to return to the house. Libby and Ab came up separately sometime later. In fact it was three hours before Libby returned to the house. No explanation was ever given for where she was during that time. W.E. Fulcher testified that it was about 12:30 when Mrs. Reynolds walked into the basement yard. She was wearing her red-and-white flannel pajamas, and there was a grass stain on her right knee.

Ab testified at the inquest that upon her return, Smith and Libby went upstairs to Ab's room. He claimed he saw the couple go into his room from his position in the reception room and he could hear them talking. When asked why they were in his room, Ab said that Smith had probably gone there to look at the world globe because he planned to fly around the world. Ab then said that Smith came back downstairs and they talked for a while before Smith gave him his wallet. Because he was still in his swimming suit, Ab put the wallet beside a cushion on the couch. Ab then stated that Smith went back upstairs and that it was about ten minutes later when Miss Yurka called to him to say that she had heard a scream. He told authorities that he rushed upstairs and that he and Libby had found Smith lying on the bed. When asked if he had seen a gun, Ab replied, "No, sir. I never did see the gun."

The first article that appeared in the newspaper contradicted Ab's statements. He was reported to have said that he "heard what he thought to be the muffled report of a gun and then heard Mrs. Reynolds cry out that her husband had been shot."

At 1:00 a.m., Ab telephoned for an ambulance, but before it arrived, he, Libby and Yurka dragged Smith out into the hall, down the stairs and put him in a car. They raced to Baptist Hospital and arrived at 1:10 a.m. Reynolds was taken to the operating room, but there was nothing the surgeons could do to save his life. He was pronounced dead at 5:25 a.m.

A hysterical Libby was put to bed in a hospital room. Ab entered her room and ordered the nurse to leave. The nurse heard Ab say to Libby, "Don't talk. Don't say anything to anybody!"

Ab insisted that he must return to Reynolda and Wharton, a Reynolda employee, drove him there. Ab's reason was he was afraid someone would enter the house and he wanted to get rid of the whiskey glasses and whiskey, since this was during the Prohibition era. Perhaps his reason was actually to replace the gun at the scene of the crime, wiped clean of fingerprints. Several searches had been conducted already without finding the gun.

When word of Smith's death spread, several people rushed to the home of Will N. Reynolds, who lived in a mansion on Fifth Street. Clinton Hall, who lived across the street in Gray Court Apartments, recalled people banging on the door to tell Reynolds the news of his nephew's death.

Sheriff Transou Scott was not notified until 7:00 a.m. that something was wrong at Reynolda. When he arrived at the house, he was unable to talk with the major witnesses. He was told that Mrs. Reynolds had been put to bed and was under a doctor's care. Ab Walker had gone to his own home to change clothes. When the sheriff did get a chance to talk to Ab, the young man was very vague about the events just before the shooting. They talked in Ab's room. It was during their conversation that the sheriff noticed Libby's bedroom slippers under Ab's bed. Ab talked about the party and about Libby flirting with the male guests. Then Ab made a strange statement: "The truth of the matter is, Sheriff…the trouble is, Smith just thought too much of that woman." Ab did not give any further details but he did say that Smith saw Libby joking with him. Ab believed that Smith became jealous over Libby's actions at the party and stated, "When the party was over and everybody was gone, I tried to square it with him." He said that he and Smith had talked for a while in the pantry (the noise of their conversation may have been what woke Blanche Yurka the first time). Ab recalled that they shouted at each other because Smith was really angry, then he calmed down and told Ab that it wasn't his fault. After their talk, Ab stated that Smith went upstairs to join his wife. When the sheriff unexpectedly asked Ab, "Why do you think she did it?" the young man was startled. He covered his face with his hands and sobbed, "Damn it, that's something I'll take to my grave!"

Missing Gun Is Found

Several searches were made by Stewart Warnken, the estate manager, to find the weapon that had killed Smith Reynolds. Ab Walker had returned to the house supposedly to "tidy up." On his way back to the hospital, Wharton asked Ab if he knew where the gun was. The young man replied that it was up there in Smith's room. Warnken, together with R.E. Lasater and Deputy Sheriff

Barnes, searched again. This time, the gun was found on a rug in a corner of the bedroom in which Smith had been found shot through the head. The newspaper reported that the officers had searched for the gun four times, and finally found it the fifth time "lying in a prominent place." It was impossible to have overlooked it the other four times. It had simply not been there earlier.

The speculation was that Ab Walker had returned from the hospital for the sole purpose of putting the gun back in the room. Where it had been and why it had disappeared were two questions that were never answered.

THE FUNERAL

Two days later, Zachary Smith Reynolds was buried. The *Winston-Salem Journal* reported that the funeral services for the Reynolds heir would be conducted at 11:00 a.m. at the Reynolda estate, with burial following in the Salem Cemetery, Winston-Salem. Smith's relatives, except his brother Dick, arrived by train and plane for the services. Dick Reynolds was off the coast of South Africa on his freighter-yacht.

The newspaper reported that while the coroner, Dr. W.N. Dalton, had ruled the death a suicide, an inquest might be held later. The paper also stated that "nearly every person present in the house when the shooting occurred…declined to be interviewed." People who were close to the family could think of no reason Smith would have had for committing suicide. He had planned to return to school at New York University.

There was speculation about who would inherit Smith Reynolds's money. Some believed Libby would inherit nothing. The will of R.J. Reynolds Sr., who died in 1918, made no provisions for the spouses of his children in the event of death. Although Smith was given a generous allowance, he could not inherit the bulk of his father's bequest until he was twenty-eight years old.

Will N. Reynolds, who had just arrived in Winston-Salem from Cleveland, Ohio, and R.E. Lasater, Smith's guardians, granted an interview with the newspapers. Mr. Reynolds declined to speculate on the cause of death because he had not had an opportunity to talk with the widow. Lasater, on the other hand said, "From the evidence in the case, there is every reason to believe that Smith committed suicide." This same article also stated that both Mr. and Mrs. Smith Reynolds were lying on a bed on the sleeping porch when the shot was fired. Previous accounts had stated that Mrs. Reynolds was in the room but did not see the shot fired.

ILLEGAL INQUEST HELD

The sheriff called an inquest immediately after the funeral. Although state law mandated that an inquest be open to the public, the time and day of the inquest was kept secret, supposedly to keep away the mob of reporters. The *Journal* stated that the coroner had called four to testify: Libby Holman Reynolds, Dr. Fred M. Hanes, Albert Walker and Miss Blanche Yurka.

The key witness, Mrs. Libby Holman Reynolds, claimed that she "did not remember a single occurrence of the entire day and night Tuesday, July 5, with the exception of a flash when she heard Smith call her name, saw a gun in his hand and saw him fall to the floor." She contradicted earlier statements when she said the only thing she could remember was seeing Smith with a pistol to his head and hearing a shot. Libby did reveal that her husband had failed in his attempt to have sex with her on two nights. She claimed that he was very worried about that and he had urged her to "get out and have an affair with another man." When she refused to comply, she claimed Smith said, "I will have to do something to break up our marriage if you won't do that." Libby claimed she told him that sex was "a very little part of our love. The rest of our love is so big and so great that it doesn't make any difference." Libby also denied drinking or taking any drug that could account for her blackout of the events. Were these statements true or was Libby simply providing a valid reason for Smith to have committed suicide?

Blanche Yurka, Libby's theatrical friend, told the officers that she was awakened twice. The first time she thought she heard two men talking in the kitchen or the pantry below her bedroom. She got up and went downstairs thinking that Libby might be in the kitchen. The only person she encountered was Ab Walker in his bathing suit. He claimed that he was "locking up." Blanche returned to her bedroom and went back to sleep. She was awakened again by the sound of someone crying hysterically. Again, she got up and hurried down the hall toward the balcony that surrounded the living room. She again saw Ab and told him she had heard someone crying. He looked at Blanche for a moment, then he ran up the stairs. The next thing she saw was Libby and Ab dragging the body of a man down the hallway.

Ab's testimony at the inquest was often contradictory and therefore questionable. He could not explain why he had made the statement that he knew something he could never tell, something that he would carry with him to his grave. When questioned, Ab said, "I have no idea why I made that statement." Neither could he explain why Libby's bedroom slippers were found under his bed.

The rest of the guests were called to testify. These included Miss Virginia Dunklee, Mrs. William Vaught, Lewin McGinnes, James Shepherd, Charles E. Norfleet and C.G. Hill. The servants and other estate officials were also questioned, but none had any information of value except W.E. Fulcher, the guard on duty that night, who testified that he thought a noise he heard was a gunshot. He said it was about 12:45 when he heard the noise and he went to investigate.

After three days of testimony, the coroner's jury ruled out suicide and found that Zachary Smith Reynolds had died "at the hands of a party or parties unknown."

An unsubstantiated rumor has since circulated that Smith contracted a venereal disease that left him impotent. This probably has little basis, since he fathered a child with Anne Cannon, his first wife, and later with Libby, who was pregnant at the time of the death of her husband. If he was impotent, who was the father of Libby's baby? He and Ab also reportedly had spent the night in a hotel with two prostitutes.

In an attempt to convince the officials that Smith had committed suicide, Libby produced two short notes that he had written years before his actual death. The first was a short will written before he married Libby, and the second was a note he had scribbled while at Woodberry Forest School, in Virginia, dated June 1927: "My girl has turned me down. Good-by forever. Give my love to Mary, Virginia, Nancy, Dick, etc. Good-bye, cruel world—Smith."

INDICTMENT OF AB AND LIBBY

When Dick Reynolds finally arrived in Winston-Salem on August 23, six weeks after the death of his brother, he did not believe the death was a suicide. The night of his arrival, the body of Smith Reynolds was exhumed to undergo a "secret autopsy." The autopsy was to determine the entrance and exit wounds. The same doctors who had treated Smith in the hospital before he died performed the autopsy. None of them was a forensic pathologist or an expert in examining gunshot wounds. Their efforts were hampered further by the work of the embalmers. Very little information was gained by the autopsy. However, the next morning Dick Reynolds told reporters that his brother had not committed suicide.

Carlisle Higgins stated that the autopsy confirmed the testimony Dr. Hanes gave at the inquest—that the bullet had been fired "at close range" and that it had entered the right temple, then ranged downward to exit behind his left ear. Dr. Hanes was not specific as to what distance "close range" meant.

Dick Reynolds began to exert pressure on local law enforcement officers and the case was heard before the grand jury. An indictment was handed down on August 3 stating that Elizabeth Holman Reynolds and Albert Walker "did unlawfully, willfully, feloniously, premeditatedly…wound and murder Z. Smith Reynolds." Both were to be arrested and held without bail for their appearance at the October term of court. Ab was taken to the jail, but Libby had already left the state of North Carolina. Ab soon was released on $25,000 bond, and Libby's father, who was also an attorney, made a deal with the Forsyth County officials that allowed her to give herself up at Wentworth if she could also be released on the same amount of bail as Ab.

Shortly after the autopsy, Libby made a statement that was published in the *New York Sun* on September 24, 1932. She confided to reporter Ward Moorehouse, "I didn't shoot Smith. God in Heaven knows that. The Reynolds family knows it in their hearts. I loved Smith as I never loved anyone before or ever will again." She also revealed the fact that she was to have his child and that gave her something to live for. She emphasized the fact that Smith was never without a pistol and that he had threatened to kill himself on many occasions. (Smith's threats to commit suicide were not substantiated by anyone else.) He was obsessed with the fear of being kidnapped and held for ransom, so he slept with a gun on the table beside the bed. She spoke of how Smith feared she would leave him. "Smith was morbid," she said, "and because of his morbidity and because of his strange delusions, I'd often sit up with him until 6 o'clock in the morning, arguing and pleading." According to Libby, Smith even vowed to give up flying in order to devote all his time to her. Undoubtedly, Libby's interview was an attempt to influence public opinion in her favor before the upcoming trial.

Murder Charges Dropped

Suddenly, the Reynolds family reversed their demands that Ab and Libby be prosecuted. William N. Reynolds, Smith's uncle, wrote Solicitor Higgins advising him that the Reynolds family would be "quite happy if it should be your decision to drop the cases." The letter was vague, and while it acknowledged it was unlikely that Smith had committed suicide, Will Reynolds did not believe there was sufficient evidence that his nephew was murdered.

Subsequently, when the case against Libby and Ab was about to be tried, Higgins requested a nolle prosequi in the case. This left the door open for subsequent trials if new evidence was discovered. The judge complied and Mrs. Reynolds and Ab Walker were discharged and released from their appearance bonds.

Libby claimed she was not entirely happy with the charges being dropped. She wanted to be cleared of all charges, but because she was never tried and acquitted, Libby lived the remainder of her life under a cloud of suspicion. She did not need to work because she had been awarded $750,000 from Smith's estate and her child had received another $2,000,000. Over the next few years, she performed occasionally in nightclubs and did some small concerts. Offers to do another Broadway musical were not forthcoming.

After the death of her husband, Libby eventually returned to the stage to perform in *Revenge with Music* (November 28, 1934–May 27, 1935) and *You Never Know*, a musical play (September 21, 1938–November 26, 1938). She is not credited with any more Broadway performances until she produced and performed in *Blues, Ballads and Sin-Songs*. It ran only two weeks, from October 4 to October 16, 1954.

UNPROVEN THEORIES

In the 1980s, several books about Libby Holman and the death of her husband appeared in print. Author Milt Machlin described in great detail Libby's life before she met Smith Reynolds and the many tragedies that occurred in her life afterward. He concludes that because Libby was Jewish, her reputation had been maligned by the people in North Carolina, especially the law enforcement officers. Neither did he believe that either Ab Walker or Libby Holman Reynolds shot Smith Reynolds. Machlin points out the many discrepancies recorded in the transcript of the inquest (of which only one incomplete copy existed with several pages missing). However, Machlin does hypothesize that either Smith found his wife and his friend Ab Walker in some compromising position or that they invited him to join them in a threesome. Libby had been in Ab's room; her bedroom slippers were found under his bed. Both Ab and Libby had been drinking heavily all night and Libby may have taken some drugs. According to Libby, Smith had frequently threatened to kill himself and was often depressed and in a black mood. Machlin did not believe that Smith was impotent because he had fathered a child by Anne Cannon and Libby had become pregnant. Current DNA testing could have proved whether Smith was the father of the baby or not.

Another possibility is that Libby took off some of her clothes downstairs and left them on the couch. Smith followed her upstairs. She took off the rest of her clothes and dropped her striped red jersey on the bathroom floor. She then put on her peach negligee and slippers. She and Smith had an argument (which Blanche Yurka heard). Libby stalked off and went to Ab's room, either to talk, make love or to ask Ab to join them. Machlin believes that Smith, "despondent and confused," returned to their room (or perhaps he never left it) and shot himself. Hearing the shot, Libby and Ab ran into Smith's bedroom and found him. She left her bedroom slippers in Ab's room.

Machlin did not believe that either Ab Walker or Smith Reynolds were homosexuals. They were probably both appalled by Libby's lifestyle, while in love with her at the same time.

Smith may have learned that he was incapable of satisfying Libby's sexual appetites, which involved bizarre, unusual and bisexual activities. With the optimism of youth, he thought that his love for her would solve all their marital problems, but it did not and could not.

PERRY'S HYPOTHESIS

Hamilton Darby Perry, author of *Libby Holman: Body and Soul*, proposed that the angle at which the bullet entered Reynolds's head would rule out suicide. He also included a sketch of the positions of the "murderer" and his "victim" that would account for the location of the bullet fragments, the shell casing and the marks made on the bed as the bullet ricocheted before hitting the window.

In the scenario Perry envisions, Smith went outside then returned to the house to find Libby and Ab Walker together. Smith was in a very black mood. He knew his relationship with Libby was deteriorating, but he feared he was losing her. If he had learned that she was pregnant, he might have worried that the baby was not his. These facts alone would lead one to believe that he had committed suicide, but did he?

Perry believed that Smith followed a trail of Libby's clothes that led from the living room to Ab's bedroom. When he found the couple, Libby was probably naked. With his jealous disposition, that alone could have enflamed Smith to the point that he might have attacked Ab. Perry believes that there was a struggle for the gun that Smith always carried and that the gun was accidentally fired. Perry does not state equivocally whether Ab or Libby fired the fatal shot, and he contradicts himself with his diagram, which depicted the person holding the gun standing at the end of the bed several feet away from Smith, who was near the head of the bed on the side that faced the outside wall.

Astrologist's Theory

The most bizarre theories came from an astrologist who wrote Sheriff Scott to say that while he was in a trance he saw a man drive up to the Reynolds home in a car that carried a New York or New Jersey license plate. He envisioned a man getting out of the car and entering the house. The astrologist claimed he saw the man shoot Smith Reynolds and then the man fled. This seems unlikely but there was a similar story told by Kramer, the tutor. He said he went outside about 11:15 and saw Smith wandering around the grounds. Kramer noticed a strange car approach the house from the north side of the back drive, the road used by servants and delivery trucks. The car stopped near the house and cut its headlights. Smith saw it and went inside for a large flashlight. When Smith returned, the car backed around and left the way it had come, still with the headlights off. Neither the car nor the driver was ever identified.

My own theory is that either Libby or Ab struggled with Smith when he put the gun to his head in a suicide attempt. Their efforts failed and, as a result, the gun went off and Smith was fatally wounded. Libby and Ab were stunned. The pair stood paralyzed for several minutes. They tried to stop the flow of blood with some towels. Ab ran downstairs to use the telephone to call an ambulance. While he was downstairs, Blanche Yurka looked over the balcony to tell Ab she had heard a shot. Ab then ran back upstairs without telling Blanche that he already knew Smith had been shot.

UNANSWERED QUESTIONS

Did Smith Reynolds commit suicide? Or did Ab Walker shoot his friend in self-defense when Smith caught Ab with Libby? Was Ab simply trying to stop his friend Smith from committing suicide?

Ab never admitted being in the room when the gun went off. Why did he not say he was there and that he tried to stop Smith from committing suicide? Perhaps he could not admit that he was in the room because it would implicate Libby somehow. Or perhaps he feared he would be charged with murder.

Or was it Libby who, in a drunken haze, had fired the fatal shot? One author tends to believe that she was so drunk she did not even know whether she had killed her husband or not and that lack of knowledge haunted her the rest of her life.

A complete autopsy was never performed on the body of Smith Reynolds. Today, skin tests of his hand would have settled the question as to whether he had fired the gun himself. Polygraph tests could have determined who was telling the truth and who was lying. Sadly, none of these things were available at the time, so after nearly seventy-five years, the death of Zachary Smith Reynolds remains a mystery. Perhaps the truth was the secret that Ab Walker told Sheriff Scott he was "going to take to my grave."

Answers to a number of questions were not forthcoming either during the inquest or the grand jury hearing. If answered, they might have solved the mystery. Who took the gun and when and why was it returned? What did Ab and Smith do on the night of July 4, which they spent in the hotel room? Did Libby really have amnesia for the entire day or did she simply claim not to remember to protect herself or someone else? Where did Smith find Libby when he went upstairs? Was she alone or with Ab Walker? If it was suicide, why did Smith Reynolds kill himself? Why did the Reynolds family drop the charges against Ab Walker and Libby Reynolds? Who was in the car that drove up to the house about 11:15, stopped and turned off the lights before leaving the way it had come? Were the occupants of that car Jim Shepard and Mrs. Vaugh or an unknown person who had no business being on the grounds? Was Smith Reynolds left-handed or right-handed? The tutor testified that Smith wrote with his right hand, but his shooting friends stated he always shot a gun with his left hand. The answer to this question alone would have made the differentiation between murder and suicide easy to determine.

After the Reynolds family made it known that they did not want charges pressed against Ab Walker and Libby Holman Reynolds, the investigation was dropped. The Reynolds family may not have wanted to incur any more scandal, especially once it was evident that Libby was pregnant. Although they did not want the taint of suicide attached to Smith Reynolds, the alternative was even worse—that his friend or his wife had murdered him. A trial might have brought out the truth, but in the process, many things that should remain private would also have been aired in public.

Life Goes On for Libby

Libby Holman Reynolds earned fame and fortune as a torch singer in the 1920s and 1930s for her steamy songs. She is credited with the invention of the strapless evening gown. She contributed to the civil rights movement and helped finance the visit of Martin Luther King Jr. to India to meet with Mahatma Ghandi. Libby did her part to fight against bigotry and racism with her songs, which helped diminish the difference between black and white singers.

Libby used her money from the estate of Z. Smith Reynolds to build a mansion in Connecticut. In the 1940s and 1950s, Libby hosted fabulous parties on her estate, attended by such famous guests as Elizabeth Taylor, Mike Todd, Truman Capote, Tennessee Williams, Roddy McDowell, Imogene Coca and Martha Raye.

Libby's Second Marriage

Libby began dating Phillip Holmes about 1938. He resembled Smith Reynolds in many ways, and he also was very jealous and insecure. Phillip joined the Royal Canadian Air Force and entrusted his intended bride to his brother Ralph. The younger brother was also a pilot and an actor as well, though not very successful. While Phillip was away, Libby and Ralph—who was twelve years younger than she—eloped. After a brief honeymoon in Florida, the newlyweds returned to live at Libby's estate in Connecticut.

The newspapers insinuated that Ralph might be homosexual. Clifton Webb commented, "He's too beautiful to be straight." A few months after their marriage, on November 11, 1939, Libby was finally able to take possession of the $750,000 awarded her from her husband's estate. In the meantime, Ralph received his draft notice but got a deferment on the grounds that he had to support his wife. That all changed after Libby inherited the money from the estate. Then Ralph got the news that his brother Phillip had been killed in the Battle of Britain. Guilt-ridden for marrying his brother's girl, Ralph volunteered.

Ralph returned from the war a changed man in 1945, and they agreed to separate. They met with her lawyer and signed a legal separate agreement. Libby was then called away to Cincinnati because her father was ill. When she returned, she was shocked to learn that her husband, Ralph Holmes, had been found dead in his apartment. He had apparently been dead for about eight days, and the body was bloated. The police determined that the cause of death was alcohol and barbiturates. Some speculated that Ralph was despondent over his separation from Libby and had committed suicide, but no note was ever found. It was also a mystery who had discovered the body, although the medical examiner's office told a newspaper that Libby had found him. There was never any question over Libby's involvement in her second husband's death. She had a solid alibi—she was in Cincinnati at the time he died.

Tragedy Follows Libby

Libby's son, Christopher "Topper" Smith Reynolds, was born prematurely on January 10, 1933. He died while mountain climbing in 1952. Christopher was attempting to climb the eastern face of Mount Whitney. His companion, Steve Wasserman, was found first about fifteen hundred feet lower down the mountain than Reynolds. Searchers determined that Topper had fallen about four hundred feet before getting stuck in a crevice. Libby was devastated by the unexpected death of her beloved son.

On June 18, 1971, Libby was found dead. Her death was ruled as a suicide from carbon monoxide. Some questions were raised because the ignition of the Rolls Royce had been turned off and the motor was not running when she was found wearing only a bathing suit.

By the time of her death, Libby had gained notoriety not only as a torch singer and actress, but also as a civil rights activist and conservationist.

What Became of Ab Walker

Rumors circulated around Winston-Salem that Ab Walker got drunk one night at the country club and told those near him that he had shot Smith Reynolds. It was also rumored that Ab was actually the father of Christopher Smith Reynolds.

After Ab Walker received $50,000 from the estate of Z. Smith Reynolds, he moved to the Southwest. He lived quietly and without attracting attention and he died of a terminal illness. After the day the inquest was held, Ab never saw, spoke or wrote to Libby Holman Reynolds.

Something Good From Something Bad

In memory of her son, Libby set up the Christopher Reynolds Foundation, a private grant-making foundation that principally supports innovative work toward international peace, disarmament, civil rights and opposes racism.

When Libby died, her home, Treetops, and surrounding property were offered to the town of Stamford, Connecticut. Town officials declined to accept the property because of the high cost of maintenance. In 2000, Treetops was sold for $11.5 million dollars to International Paper. The company retains the use of the thirty-three-room mansion as a conference center. The grounds are famous for the wide variety of trees, shrubs, vines, herbs and other plants.

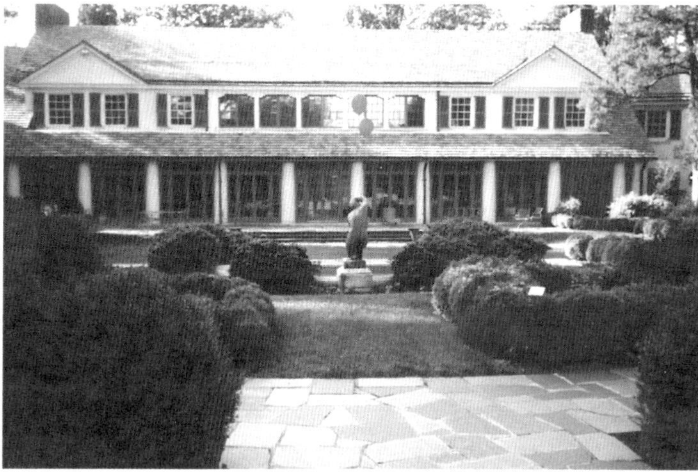

Reynolda House, once home of Z. Smith Reynolds and the site of his untimely death. *Photography by Frances H. Casstevens.*

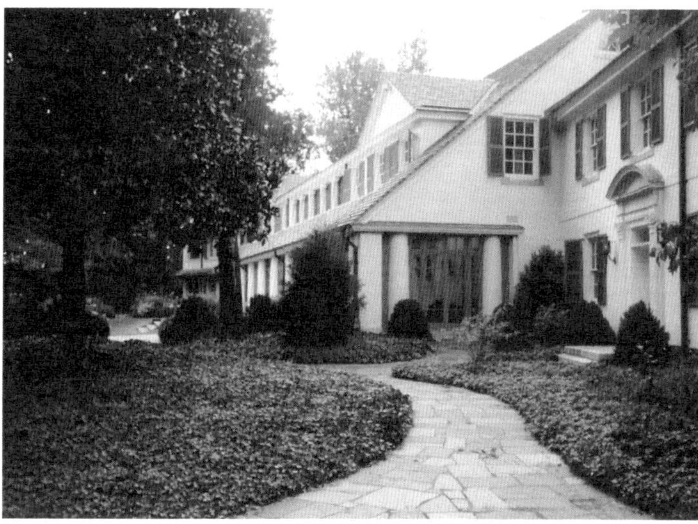

Smith Reynolds died in an upstairs room in this wing of the house. *Photography by Frances H. Casstevens.*

Reynolda House

Reynolda, the grand Reynolds home, was opened to the public in 1965 as the Reynolda House Museum of American Art. The art collection ranges from the colonial period to the present. Outside the house, visitors can tour a formal garden. Many of the original outbuildings now serve as shops, art galleries and restaurants. The quiet serenity of the grounds, only a few yards from a busy street, are reminiscent of the scene greeted by Dorothy in the *Wizard of Oz* when she steps out of her house and everything is in color rather than black and white.

In 1997 the house and grounds were featured in one of the episodes of *America's Castles*, a presentation of the A&E Television Network.

Thousands of visitors tour Reynolda House and grounds each year. They are impressed by the fine art and furnishings and the magnificent grounds with its beautiful flowers. Few of today's visitors know that this house was the scene of the mysterious death of Zachary Smith Reynolds.

The siblings of Zachary Smith Reynolds used their share of his estate to start the Z. Smith Reynolds Foundation, which has been a major force for the achievement of worthy projects throughout the South. The Z. Smith Reynolds Foundation was instrumental in the relocation of Wake Forest College to Winston-Salem, where it is now the outstanding Wake Forest University. A portrait of Smith Reynolds by artist Joe King was unveiled in the spring of 1964 in the Z. Smith Reynolds Library at Wake Forest University, named in his honor.

TRAGEDY IMMORTALIZED ON FILM

In 1939, *Reckless*, a motion picture starring Jean Harlow, was a thinly veiled story about the Reynolds murder. In 1956 Universal International Pictures again used the story as the basis for the motion picture *Written on the Wind*, starring Rock Hudson and Lauren Bacall. Other major roles were filled by Robert Stack and Dorothy Malone. Although the names were changed in the film, the story was still recognizable as the Reynolds tragedy. Both movies are currently available on DVD.

A stage adaptation by Sky Gilbert of the Holman and Reynolds story entitled *Play Murder* premiered in 1993. It was revived in October of 2003 and opened at the Buddies in Bad Times Theater in Toronto, Canada. The play addressed some lingering questions: Was Libby planning to murder Smith for his money? Did she find him inadequate when compared to her lesbian lovers? Was Reynolds impotent and did this cause him to commit suicide?

As recently as 1994, the Reynolds tragedy was summarized by Frank V. Tursi in *Winston-Salem: A History*. The story continues to intrigue us.

A Stokes County Tragedy: The Lawson Family Murders

Sometime we'll understand.

Christmas in 1929 was a sad year for almost everyone. After the stock market crashed on October 29, 1929, the bad news continued. The *Greensboro News* reported a number of tragic events in their issue of December 26. The lead story was about Charlie Lawson, a Stokes County farmer, who murdered his wife and six children before killing himself on Christmas Day. Another front-page story was that of three fliers who were killed when their plane crashed near Dunn, North Carolina. In that same issue was the news about the murder of a prominent Knoxville physician, his wife and his nephew. In Wisconsin, three members of a family were killed when their automobile was struck by a train. In Paris, three black children were burned to death. In Kentucky, a mob broke a prisoner out of jail, shot him five times and then threw his body over a cliff. A black woman was shot in Charlotte, North Carolina, and a New York boy was killed on a sled he had received as a Christmas present.

Indeed, it was a sad Christmas for many people, including the friends and neighbors of the Lawson family, a Christmas that many remembered as long as they lived.

Events Leading up to the Murder

In 1929 Charlie Lawson was a forty-three-year-old farmer who was respected by his friends, family and throughout the community. He was a member of the Germanton Lodge. Lawson was regarded as an honest man, according to one newspaper report, and a good provider for his family. He did not rent or sharecrop but was in the process of paying for his farm. He had plans to build a new house once the land was paid for. The Charlie Lawson farm consisted of

128 acres on Brook Cove Road near Germanton, North Carolina, and its cash crop was tobacco.

Some months before the murders, Charlie dug a basement for his pack house. Then he had to dig a drainage ditch so that water could escape from under the building. As he swung his mattock, it struck something and rebounded to hit Charlie in the head. The injury was severe enough that Charlie visited Dr. Helsabeck in Germanton. Several blood vessels had been cut on the wounded man's scalp and he had two black eyes for several weeks, but Dr. Helsabeck stated after the murders that Charlie's injury was not severe enough to have caused him to commit such horrible deeds.

Charlie Lawson apparently recovered from his accident, but some of the people who knew him said that he was changed afterward. They said he would walk away in the middle of a conversation with a friend. He also had some sort of painful growth (cancerous?) on his chest. According to Bruce Jones, that growth was about the size of "two hands laid side by side." A friend remembered Charlie saying a few months before the murders, "I wouldn't mind dying if I could only take my family with me…"

Neighbors, friends and relatives recalled that there had been frequent family fights and that Charlie had made threats of violence against his family. Sometime in the fall of 1928, a year before the murders, Charlie was involved in a fight with a black man, an employee of the warehouse. The man ran a cart into Charlie's leg twice, and the second time, Charlie attacked the black man. The black man pulled a knife and sliced Charlie several times, then escaped. Although injured, Charlie followed the man until he collapsed outside the warehouse on the sidewalk. Charlie was taken to a hospital where he remained for two weeks.

Just before he murdered his family, Charlie did something out of character and totally unexpected—he took his whole family to Winston-Salem, bought them new outfits and had their picture made in their new clothes. He also purchased some trinkets and toys for the children. It is this group photograph that appeared in the newspapers. As shown in the photograph, the Lawsons were a handsome family. Was Charlie already planning to murder his family? Were the murders premeditated?

DECEMBER 25, 1929

A six-inch snow had covered the ground several days before Christmas. Because the temperature remained cold, much of the snow was still on the ground. Rabbits were plentiful and easy to track in the snow, so some of the Lawson men decided to hunt rabbits after the noon meal. Arthur Lawson, Charlie's sixteen-year-old son, wanted to hunt as well but he did not have shells (although his father had plenty). So Arthur and his cousin, Sanders Lawson, walked to the store in Germanton to buy some. By mid-afternoon, Claude Lawson decided to visit his uncle Charles and his family. If Claude and his father, Elijah Lawson, had heard any shots coming from the Charlie Lawson cabin, they assumed someone was also hunting rabbits. Claude Lawson, who was still living in 1977, told reporter Glenna Hicks that he bounded up the steps to the cabin and opened the door upon the scene of the massacre before him. In 1977 Claude could not recall the position of the bodies but he remembered all the blood. He remembered thinking that whoever killed the family could still be upstairs, so he and his father left the house and ran for help.

The Bloody Crimes

Accounts of the murders in the papers stated that the killing had begun in the house. On the ground floor inside the house, Mrs. Lawson was shot while holding her five-month-old girl. One of the little boys had been washing his face when he was shot. The other little boy and Marie, the oldest child, were both killed in the main room of the house. It was believed that the two little girls, Carrie and Maybelle, had run away from the crime scene and were killed by their father as they passed the tobacco barn on their way to another relative's house. After he was sure the girls were dead, Charlie put them in the tobacco barn and crossed their hands on their chests and placed a stone under their heads for a pillow.

Charlie then arranged the bodies of his other victims on the floor in the house, and he put a pillow under each of their heads. He put the baby back in its crib. Then he left the house and went into the woods. Much later, after law officers had arrived, the shot was heard when Charlie killed himself.

The victims were Mrs. Fannie Manring Lawson, age thirty-eight, and her six children: Marie, sixteen; Carrie, thirteen; Maybelle, ten; James, seven; Raymond, five; and Mary Lou, five months. The oldest son, Arthur, escaped with his life. He was not at home when the killings occurred.

The clock on the mantle had stopped at 1:25 p.m. Some thought perhaps Lawson had stopped the clock himself, while others believed that the jar caused by blasts from his shotgun had upset the mechanism and caused it to stop.

The Funeral

The bodies of the Lawson family were taken to a funeral home in Madison. The funeral home was unprepared to handle eight bodies at the same time. They had only six white coffins in which to place the family, so Charlie was buried in a gray one. They also had to improvise and used a piano stool and a small table to hold two of the children's caskets for the viewing of the bodies.

The *Winston-Salem Journal* ran a lengthy article that included a picture showing the caskets and some of the crowd. Because of bad road conditions, the burial was delayed until December 27.

It was estimated that five thousand people attended the funeral for the eight Lawson family victims. All were buried side by side in the same grave at the Browder Cemetery not far from their home. There was no church at this cemetery and no church service was held. The Junior Order of the United American Mechanics, of which Charlie was a member, took charge of the burial. A large common grave was dug for seven coffins. The baby was placed in the coffin with its mother. After a short service, the coffins were opened and relatives, friends and curiosity-seekers filed by for three hours to view the bodies.

The monument erected at the Lawson graves carried the inscription, "Not now, but in the coming years, it will be a better land: We will read the meaning of our tears and then, sometime, we'll understand."

AUTOPSY PERFORMED

No one could understand what had happened to Charlie to make him so crazy as to kill his family and himself. Some of the friends and relatives of Charlie Lawson thought that the blow to his head several months earlier might have affected his brain. Dr. Helsabeck, a local doctor, was quoted in a Winston-Salem paper saying that "The convolutions on the top of the brain [of Charlie Lawson] near the middle vary from side to side from those on either side." All had hoped the autopsy would reveal the cause of Charlie's behavior, but even Dr. Spotswood Taylor, a surgeon at Johns Hopkins, could find no abnormalities. Years later, Dr. Taylor indicated that he saw nothing unusual or remarkable in the brain of Charlie Lawson. Charlie's brain was sent to Johns Hopkins Hospital in Baltimore, Maryland, for further examination. No abnormalities were found.

Still, some of the Lawson relatives believed that Charlie must have sustained brain damage from the blow to his head when he was hit by a mattock. After that incident, Charlie complained of bad headaches for about a year. His nephew Claude Lawson remembered Charlie's wife saying that her husband would be "sitting there at night and would jump up and see if all of his guns were loaded."

In his pockets at the time of his death, Charlie had several bills of sale for tobacco. On the back of one of those bills, he had scribbled, "Blame no one but I." On another, he had written, "Trouble will cause." Yet neither of the notes gave any reason why Charlie had killed his family.

Shockwaves from the Tragedy

The neighbors and family of the Lawsons were shocked. Nothing like this tragedy had ever occurred in Stokes County or even in the surrounding counties of the Piedmont section of North Carolina.

Because of the newspaper publicity, the crime was known throughout the state. The curiosity seekers came in droves to visit the crime scene. Because of the large numbers who wanted to see for themselves the place where the murders occurred, relatives of the Lawson family erected a fence around the property, and one of the more enterprising relatives began charging a fee for admission. A resident of nearby Walnut Cove stated that on one day he counted twenty automobiles parked in front of the Lawson home.

The lone survivor, Arthur Lawson, did not return to his home, but moved in with one of his uncles.

Immortalized in Song and Poetry

Almost immediately after news of the murders was made known, poems and songs were written about the tragedy. A poem by Edith Willard entitled "The Lawson Tragedy in Rhyme" appeared in *The Yadkin Ripple*, a paper published in an adjoining county.

Quite a number of folk and bluegrass musicians have kept the story of the Lawson family murder alive. Probably the first recording was made by the Carolina Buddies entitled "Murder of the Lawson Family." Another early musician, Wade Mainer, recorded "Charlie Lawson." Other artists who have recorded the song include Spence Moore, Glen Neaves, George Pegram and Red Parham and Walter "Kid" Smith. Some of the more recent musicians and better known to the current generation to have recorded the story are Doc and Merle Watson ("Lawson Family Murder"), Mac Wiseman ("The Ballad of the Lawson Family"), the Country Gentlemen ("The Story of Charlie Lawson"), the Stanley Brothers ("Ballad of Charlie Lawson") and Charlie Poole ("Ballad of the Lawson Family").

Arthur Lawson, the sole survivor of the tragedy, also met a tragic end. He never got over the loss of his whole family, but eventually he married and he and his wife had four children. His life was cut short when at age thirty-five, he was killed in a truck accident.

THE TRUTH WILL OUT

A full account of the tragedy and the events leading up to it was published in 1990. The book, written by M. Bruce Jones and his daughter, Trudy J. Smith, was appropriately titled *White Christmas, Bloody Christmas*.

By talking with family members and neighbors who actually saw the crime scene, the authors were able to piece together the sequence of events. Hill Hampton, who was twenty-four years old in 1929, was especially helpful because he had been there and seen the footsteps in the snow and the blood. Jones and Smith proposed that the two little girls, Carrie and Maybelle, were the first to die as they walked toward the home of their uncle, Elijah Lawson. They base their theory on the fact that the girls were fully dressed with coats and hats. If the girls had run from the house in terror, they would not have taken the time to put on their hats and coats.

The book includes many photographs of the crime scene. While it is not a scholarly work and lacks references or footnotes, the authors acknowledge a number of people they interviewed and from whom the information was obtained.

Now out of print, in the spring of 2006 a copy of *White Christmas, Bloody Christmas* was offered for sale on eBay. The bidding for this rare book reached over $300. Over the years, interest in this tragedy does not seem to wane.

What makes the book unique and sets it apart from the contemporary articles is the fact that it includes the reason Charlie Lawson murdered his family. Just

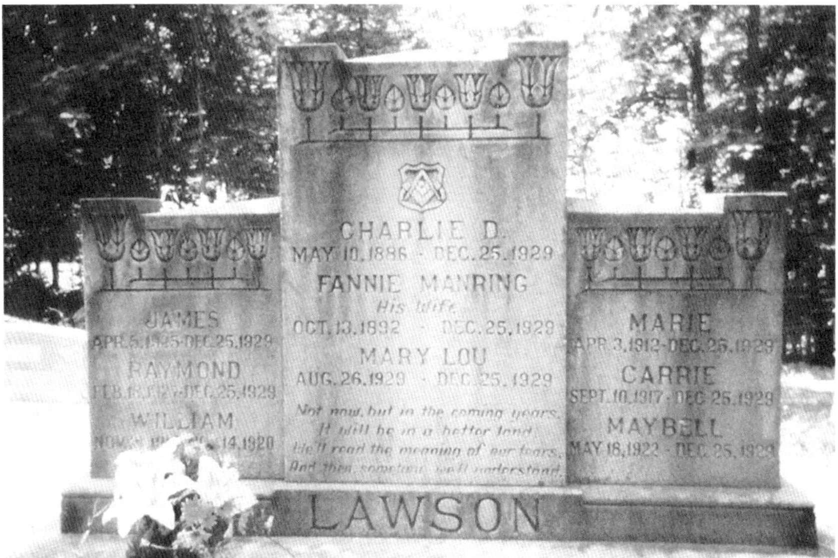

The burial site of the Lawson family in the Browder Cemetery near Walnut Cove. *Courtesy of Linda Allman.*

before the book was to be published, Stella Lawson, who was only thirteen years old in 1929, contacted Jones and Smith. She confided the reason for the murders, the truth of which she did not learn until years later when she was a grown woman. Stella said that her Aunt Nina, the wife of George Lawson, and therefore her aunt by marriage told her that Fannie Lawson had become aware some time before Christmas that her daughter Marie was pregnant. Fannie confided in her two sisters-in-law (Nina and Ida Lawson) that her daughter was pregnant and that Charlie Lawson was the father of her baby. The murders seem to have been precipitated by Marie's desire to leave home and marry another man and Charlie was becoming more violent. He had excruciating headaches and insomnia. After Stella was told this information, her Aunt Nina asked her not to repeat it.

Stella Lawson Boles kept her promise for many years, but she finally broke her vow of silence and revealed the motive for the murders before the book *White Christmas, Bloody Christmas* went to press. She was glad to have been relieved of the burden she carried so long and free of having to tell lies when she knew the truth.

Remains of the Crime Scene in 2006

Today, nothing remains of the Lawson family cabin. George Lee Watts tore down the old house and used the boards to build a covered bridge.

The curious can still visit the graves of the family in the Browder Cemetery. Esther Johnson, a member of the Surry County Historical Society of Mount Airy, North Carolina, and historical artifact collector Patrick Boyles of Winston-Salem, North Carolina, have put together a program about the Lawson family tragedy, which they present to various groups in the Piedmont area of North Carolina. Their presentation includes posters with all the newspaper articles, copies of the actual death certificates of the deceased family members and other genealogical and factual information. By the spring of 2006, Jackson and Boyles had presented their program eight times.

Otto Wood: The Bandit

They put him in the pen, but it done no good.
It wouldn't hold a man called Otto Wood.

In the days of Al Capone, Bonnie and Clyde and John Dillinger, North Carolina had its own outlaw—Otto Wood. They called him "the Houdini of Cell Block A" and, indeed, his miraculous escapes from prison rivaled the famous magician's. Wood escaped a total of ten times from prison. Four of those escapes were from the North Carolina State Prison, the rest from prisons in Tennessee and Virginia. This record was remarkable in itself, and almost miraculous considering the prisoner had only one hand and a crippled foot.

Otto's Own Account of His Crimes, Imprisonment and Escapes

While a prisoner at the North Carolina State Prison, Otto Wood, with only six months of schooling, wrote and published his autobiography, *A True History of My Life, Ranging from Four Years Old up Till the Present,* in which he details how his criminal career progressed. His motive was to let the public judge whether he was as desperate as he had been portrayed in the newspapers and possibly to generate public support during his upcoming trial for the murder of A.W. Kaplan, the Greensboro pawnbroker who died after being hit on the head by Wood. He also wanted to make his children aware of the fate of their father and hoped they would learn from his mistakes.

Wood admitted to car theft, to making and hauling whiskey and to gambling. He denied ever having been guilty of "butchery and murder, as the newspaper claimed." He declared, "There was not a man in North Carolina or any other state, who values a man's life higher than I do." And, although he was charged with Kaplan's murder, he maintained that the man died from some cause other than the "scalp wound he received in our fight."

Wood also admitted to having been in a "shooting scrape in Tennessee in 1916," but stated that he had been "exonerated from all blame." None of those injured in this shootout received fatal wounds.

Childhood and Early Life

Otto Wood was born in Wilkes County, North Carolina, in either 1892 or 1894. His life of crime began early. His father died when he was four years old, leaving Otto and four brothers, ranging from two to ten years, in the care of their widowed mother. Otto saw himself as different from his siblings. "I wanted to be going somewhere all the time and would not stay at home." When he was five years old, he would slip away to the woods and explore hollow trees and rock cliffs. He seemed to crave adventure. After age seven, Wood refused to go to school because he did not like to be confined and because the other boys made fun of his shabby clothes. When he was only seven years old, Otto ran away from home.

According to Otto, he boarded a train without a ticket. He managed to fool the conductor into thinking he was with other people. When the train reached Winston-Salem, Otto got off and walked around the town. He was impressed by the size of the city. When night came, Otto went to a tobacco warehouse and asked a farmer to give him something to eat. The farmer let the child sleep in his wagon that night. The farmer took Otto to his home in Madison where the child stayed a couple of days. Then Otto decided to move on. He boarded a train at Madison that was headed for Roanoke, Virginia. There he caught a train bound for Hagerstown, Maryland, but the conductor discovered him. When the train stopped, the conductor turned the little boy over to the police. The policemen took up a collection and bought Otto a new suit and a train ticket home.

Otto's mother notified the railroads not to let the boy ride the trains anymore. The next time he tried it, the conductor put him off. He found a way to avoid being put off by slipping into the tool box of a freight train and he made his way again to Winton-Salem. Eventually, he made it all the way to Bluefield, West Virginia. There, he was again caught and taken to the police. However, the police chief knew Otto's uncle and sent the boy on to him in Vulcan, West Virginia. Otto's uncle was running a saloon in Mingo County. His uncle lived near the Hatfields, and there was plenty of excitement provided by the Hatfield-McCoy feud. Otto made friends with some of the Hatfields and they took him to their home. Otto recalled that the Hatfields "made and drank whiskey, gambled, and had a big time generally." The boy learned to do all these things, and by the time he was ten, he was good at gambling.

First Criminal Offense and Arrest

After some months, Otto wanted to see his mother, so he returned to Wilkes County, North Carolina. A boy who lived near his mother had a bicycle. Otto had to have that bicycle. He wanted to use it to ride back to West Virginia. He stole the bicycle and started down the road. Soon, he was overtaken by the sheriff as he pushed the bike (he did not even know how to ride it). Captured by the sheriff, he was incarcerated in the Wilkesboro jail. He stayed in the jail five months before he was tried. During his time in jail, he and another prisoner planned to rob a hardware store. His fellow prisoner assured Otto that they could get some fine guns at the store. The plan suited Otto because he had "a great fancy for guns." When he did come up for trial, the judge sentenced Otto to the chain gang in Iredell County for six months. Because he was so small, the foreman of the chain gang sent him home. At the time he was sent to the chain gang, Otto could not have been older than twelve years of age.

Second Arrest

Back in Wilkes County, Otto proceeded with the plan he and his fellow prisoner had made. He robbed the hardware store and took all the guns he could carry. He was soon caught and put back in jail to be held until the next session of court. The presiding judge was Honorable Judge Allen from Goldsboro. A compassionate Christian man, the judge wanted to help Otto. The judge postponed sentencing Otto until Friday when Otto's brother could attend. The judge placed Otto in his brother's custody and instructed him not to let Otto get into any more trouble. Otto's brother told the judge that he had tried and failed, that he could do nothing with Otto. Otto's story is the opposite. His brother, Otto wrote, had always "done all he could to make life miserable for me." The judge told the brother to take Otto home to his mother and advised the young boy to stay out of trouble.

Having been convicted of a crime, Otto found that he was not welcomed anywhere. Every place he went, he was told, "Get out, you little devil." So Otto started traveling again. Occasionally he would return to West Virginia and stay a month or two with the Hatfields. Otto decided to settle down and get a job. He went to work in the coal mines as a "trapper." He continued to work in the coal mines until he was seventeen, then he got a job as a locomotive fireman for the Norfolk and Western Railway, which ran between Bluefield, West Virginia, and Williamson. It was while he was a fireman that Otto lost his hand. In his autobiography, Otto gives no details about how this occurred.

Third Arrest and First Prison Escape

No longer able to work, Otto married a girl from Point Pleasant, West Virginia. Otto was a favorite with the ladies, and another girl he had been seeing had him arrested for breach of his promise to marry her and for being the father of her child. He was arrested, tried, convicted and sentenced to two years and two months in the Virginia State Prison.

It was after this third arrest that Otto first escaped from prison, an act that he later came to view as "the biggest mistake I ever made." Chased for several days by law enforcement officers, the fugitive made his way across the mountains. He traveled to Texas, Arizona and New Mexico, living from the winnings he made gambling. He became a heavy drinker, and he always wore two big guns, as many westerners did. He was involved in some shootouts but came away unharmed. He remained in the West for two years before he decided to return to the East. As he made his way, he was recognized in Portsmouth, Ohio, arrested and returned to the Virginia State Prison. Another year was added to his sentence for escaping.

Fourth Arrest and Second Escape

Otto had only been back in prison three months when he escaped again and made his way to Chattanooga, Tennessee. Shortly after arriving there, he got into trouble gambling in a poolroom "run by colored people."

Otto was good at gambling and soon won all the money. However, the other gamblers used their guns to take Otto's winnings. A gunfight ensued. Otto had been outnumbered twenty to one, and when the smoke cleared, Otto, according to his story, was the only one left standing. The rest had either fled or were lying on the floor. Although Otto was seriously wounded in the gunfight, he was arrested for shooting three men. When he had recovered and was out of the hospital, Otto claimed "self-defense" and was released. Had he not been using the name C.H. Staley, Otto would probably have been arrested on other charges. He counted himself lucky to have gotten out of the poolroom alive and without killing anyone.

Otto left Tennessee and returned to Welch, West Virginia, where he began hauling whiskey. He bought a car on the "installment plan" and married a girl in Welch. His luck did not hold and only a few days after the wedding, he was in trouble over the whiskey. He fled with his new bride to North Carolina. The people who sold him the car telegraphed the officers in North Wilkesboro and, by the time he arrived at his mother's home, the officers were there to arrest him. Avoiding arrest, Otto made his way to Winston-Salem, leaving his car behind. There, he stole another automobile and drove back to his home in Wilkes County. This was an error on Otto's part because the officers were waiting for him. He managed to escape and took his fifteen-year-old bride with him. While the officers searched for him in the woods near his mother's house, Otto drove to Wilkesboro and stole another car. He drove to Statesville, then Charlotte, and on through South Carolina, Georgia and Florida. The tires on his stolen car began to wear out, so he stopped and stole tires from another car while its owner was asleep.

FIFTH ARREST AND THIRD ESCAPE

Out of money, Otto and his wife left Florida and traveled north. He was arrested in Winfield, Kentucky, and was taken to Chattanooga, Tennessee, to stand trial for "forcible trespass and larceny of an automobile." He bemoaned the fact that the officers did not "give him any credit for leaving the other car." He received three years in prison.

Back in prison, Otto watched for a chance to escape. He waited for six months before his chance came and he left Tennessee behind and returned to North Carolina. The news of his escape preceded him and the officers were waiting for him to show up at his mother's home. He had only been free two weeks when he was captured and returned to the Tennessee prison. The boy just did not seem to learn from his mistakes.

FOURTH ESCAPE

From the Tennessee prison, Otto escaped by hiding inside a big "dry goods box." However, he was seen as he exited the box and was chased like a "fox pursued by a pack of hounds." As the officers drew closer, Otto saw a farmhouse. He ran into the stable and stole a horse. He did not even have time to put a bridle or saddle on the horse before the officers reached the barn. When they saw that he had taken the horse, they gave up the chase. Although he eventually made his way to a town that was forty miles from Nashville, he was soon recognized and surrounded by a crowd that demanded he surrender. A fight ensued and Otto was hurt. To the doctor who examined him, he pretended to be hurt worse than he really was. After four hours, the train arrived to carry Wood back to Nashville. When they reached Union Station, he gave his guard a "rabbit punch" and escaped from him. In one of the trains, he found a pair of overalls and jumpers a flagman had left. He put the clothes on and greased his face. With great audacity, Otto joined the men searching for him. They thought he was a brakeman. He managed to get on a Louisville and Nashville freight train and made it to Hoptown, Kentucky, hundreds of miles from Nashville. He was almost caught when he got off the train when two officers approached and ordered him to throw up his hands. He made another dash for freedom amid bullets flying. He made his way to Welch where his first wife now lived.

Sixth Arrest and Fifth Escape

A warrant had been issued in Welch because Wood had absconded with the automobile on which only part of the purchase price had been paid. He was arrested and sentenced to five years in the West Virginia State Prison. The judge gave him that amount of time, not so much for car theft, but for his past record. Otto realized he had made a bad mistake, but he had no choice except to try escaping again. Now facing eleven years in prison, he began planning his next getaway.

Otto now found himself in the West Virginia State Prison, a facility from which it appeared the only escape was by going over the walls. The walls, however, were patrolled by guards carrying Winchester rifles. In order to escape, Otto needed help. He convinced a fellow inmate, a big man named James Borders, to help him break out. Borders, although only eighteen, was doing eighteen years for second-degree murder. They made their plans to escape on a day when it was snowing hard. That day came on January 3, 1919. Unnoticed, the pair of convicts climbed over the wall using ladders that were already inside the prison. Wood vividly remembered the next three days. The prison sat on the banks of the Ohio River at Moundsville and the pair had to cross the river. Thinly clad, the extremely cold weather affected them greatly. After walking about fifteen miles, they took shelter under a rock cliff where they built a fire and rested. Then, the two escapees parted company, and Borders went to Huntington, West Virginia, where he was captured thirty days later. Wood followed his previous pattern and headed for North Carolina.

A FEW MONTHS OF FREEDOM

Otto arrived in North Carolina where he found that the Spanish flu was rampant. He was able to help many of the sick and he began making moonshine whiskey in the mountains (probably of Wilkes County). He met a girl there and together they made the liquor. Wood hauled it to Winston-Salem where he got twenty dollars per gallon. He continued in this illegal activity for six months before being arrested again.

SEVENTH ARREST

Wilkes County officers arrested Otto once more and placed him in the Wilkes County jail. While they had him in custody, the county officers learned that three states were offering rewards for his capture. Since West Virginia offered the greatest reward and Otto had the most time to serve in that state, he was returned to West Virginia. His new girlfriend did not desert him and vowed she would help him escape.

Otto was desperate. He did not want to be returned to West Virginia. Somehow, while in the Wilkes County jail, he managed to obtain a gun. He did not reveal how he got it but did remark that most people believed the girl slipped it to him. That same girl talked him out of using the gun and promised to travel back to West Virginia with him. She proved good as her word, and she accompanied Deputy Warden E.W. Athey when Otto was taken to West Virginia. The girl was allowed to accompany them when she promised that she would not let Otto cause any trouble. Otto still had the gun and would not give it to her because he planned to escape his captors in Roanoke, Virginia.

When the party arrived in Winston-Salem, the deputy told Wood they would have to wait until 4:45 the next morning to catch the train. He said if Otto would promise not to escape, he would not lock him up and that they would spend the night in the hotel. Otto was so impressed by the man's kindness that he gave up his gun. Otto asked only that the girl be given credit instead of him for his good behavior.

Once at the West Virginia prison, Deputy Athey consulted the prison directors. They decided to ask the governor to pardon Wood. If the governor of West Virginia would agree, the prison officials planned to send him on to Tennessee. The West Virginia governor released Otto to Tennessee authorities, but once he arrived in Tennessee, the prison board ruled that he would have to serve thirty-six months. They would give him no time off for good behavior. The guards made life in prison very hard for Otto.

Sixth Escape and a New Life in the West

Otto began receiving letters from the girl who had given birth to his child and who had traveled with Otto when he was taken back to West Virginia. Throughout his writing, Otto never gave the names of any of his wives or girlfriends. The news of this girlfriend upset him and he escaped from the Tennessee prison again. He gave no details in his autobiography about how he escaped or when.

Otto decided to take the girl and their baby and move to the western states. He made some liquor and hauled two loads to Winston-Salem, then picked up the girl and the baby and started out west. They camped out along the way. This was probably the happiest time in his short life. He wrote, "I think that during the short months we were together is the first time in my life that I ever felt hopeful, regardless of circumstances. To have the girl and baby along made me feel like I was in a new world. We traveled for thirteen months, part of the time on the west coast, but never stayed longer than a week at any place. We would fish and hunt as we went along, and our expenses were not very heavy." During this time, Otto and his family encountered many dangerous situations along the way. He and the girl even captured three Mexicans who were wanted for murder, kidnapping and other crimes. He turned them into the sheriff of El Paso, and as a result, his picture appeared in the newspaper with a story of his heroic deed. He did not stay around to collect the reward, however, but drove to Arizona.

Eighth Arrest

Even when Otto tried to do good deeds he got in trouble. While driving through the Texas Panhandle, he saw an automobile tire lying in the road. He stopped, picked it up and took it to a garage in Sonora. The garage owner had had a number of tires stolen, and the tire Otto returned was one of them. The garage owner notified the sheriff, who chased Otto down and arrested him. The sheriff took the trio back to Sonora and began checking up on him. He did not put him in jail but locked Otto in his own car.

Otto decided he had better leave, so he filled a canteen with water, kissed the girl and the baby goodbye and started out across the desert to San Antonio. He was soon being followed by two Texas Rangers on horseback, but Otto was crafty and soon he had the Rangers at his command. He told them they had better not mistreat the girl and the baby he had left behind or he would "appear on the scene when they least expected." The bandit took their guns and water, but left them one horse and started out across the desert again. He kept thinking about the girl he had left behind and decided to return to the hotel. Looking through a window, Otto saw that she and the baby were asleep.

Otto's presence in the town was soon discovered when his horse broke away from where it was hitched and returned to the stable where it was usually kept. The sheriff was alerted and he and five deputies went to the hotel to capture Otto. Just as Otto was calling out to the girl to wake up, he heard from behind him a voice command, "Reach for the clouds." The voice came from one of the Texas Rangers he had encountered the day before. The fugitive put up his hands but ran for a car he had stolen and left the town. The officers in fast, high-powered cars chased him. He drove across the desert but could not elude his pursuers. Finally, he abandoned the car when it got stuck in a prairie dog hole and overturned. After he left the car, the officers could not find him in the dark, so they abandoned their chase.

The fugitive wandered in the desert for three days until he came to a ranch house. Then he saw a car parked along the road. As he approached, he saw that inside were "moonlight lovers." He interrupted their lovemaking and demanded they take him to San Antonio, where he was to meet the girl. The girl was not at the place they had planned to meet. However, he soon learned by reading the newspapers that his pregnant girlfriend was being held in a town called Hopes. He could not go there because he would be recognized and captured. Soon, however, the girl, who was close to her time to give birth, was released and she returned home. Otto also returned to his mother's home.

NINTH ARREST

In order to care for his girlfriend and their two children, Otto needed money. He decided to return to whiskey-making and hauling. He needed an automobile, so he went to Portsmouth, Ohio, and stole one. Within an hour, the officers had chased him down and arrested him for auto theft. He was tried, convicted and sentenced to serve two years in the Ohio State Prison. He stayed to serve the time and was released after nineteen months in June of 1923. He then returned to West Virginia.

Otto wanted to see his girl and his babies. She was staying in Winston-Salem with one of his brothers. He visited them and took the girl and the younger child back with him to West Virginia. The older child he left with his brother, but he promised to return about once a month to visit him. It was during one of these trips that Otto got in the worst trouble of his life.

TENTH ARREST—THIS TIME FOR MURDER

After visiting his child in Winston-Salem on October 1, 1923, Otto needed some money. He drove to Greensboro to pawn his watch. Two weeks later he came to retrieve it from the pawnbroker, A.W. Kaplan, who declared he had no record of any watch. Otto knew he was lying because he had seen him make a record of the item.

Otto returned to the pawnshop again on November 2 and asked Kaplan for his watch back. The pawnshop owner again denied that he had the watch and ordered Otto out of his shop. When Otto did not leave immediately, Kaplan, according to Otto, picked up a stick to hit him. Before Kaplan's blow could be executed, Otto hit Kaplan on the head with the handle of his gun. Subsequently, the gun discharged and the bullet grazed Kaplan's skin on his shoulder.

To escape capture in Greensboro, Otto got into the "touring car" of a man named De Vane and ordered him to drive out of the city. Three miles outside, Otto ordered the man to get out of the car. Otto noticed an overcoat lying in the back seat and he took it. In one of the pockets he found some money (although, at the trial, De Vane claimed that Wood stole $100 at gunpoint). Otto left Greensboro and drove to Brimwell, West Virginia. Fewer than two weeks later, on November 11, 1923, he was arrested for the murder of A.W. Kaplan. Otto was surprised because he did not know the man was dead. Otto Wood was kept for sixty days in the Mercer County jail awaiting extradition to Greensboro. To prevent him from escaping, Otto was put in double shackles on his feet, his arms were tied behind him and a rope was placed around his neck.

The *Greensboro Daily News* played up the story of the "notorious man-killer and desperado" and found him guilty before he was even tried. Soon, Otto was the talk of the whole state. Thousands of people came to see the "wild man" being held in the Guilford County jail. Otto estimated that as many as twenty thousand came to see him and probably more were turned away. At the trial, although there were two witnesses who could testify that Otto struck Kaplan in self-defense, neither was called to the witness stand. The judge believed that the murder was not premeditated, and he advised the jury to convict Otto Wood of manslaughter or second-degree murder. The jury complied, and Otto was sentenced to thirty years in the North Carolina State Prison. Otto's treasured watch was returned to him, but he lost his freedom.

Seventh Escape

Influenced by the newspaper stories that portrayed Otto as a dangerous criminal, he was not treated very well by one of the prison wardens, S.J. Busbee. After four months, Otto talked with Busbee and told him that if he "did not let up on me he might expect most anything to happen." This angered the warden and he told Wood to go ahead if he "thought it would be easy."

Otto then began planning his escape with a fellow prisoner, John Starnes. They succeeded in making one of the most daring escapes ever from the North Carolina prison. They obtained a gun and forced the foreman in the chair factory to drive them through the gates. Although the prisoners had been treated kindly by Dr. Norman, one of the prison officials, they escaped in Norman's car. They felt guilty about that and drove back to Raleigh to exchange the doctor's car for the first one they saw. This proved to be a bad decision. The car they commandeered belonged to a black man, who was convinced he had been captured by the Ku Klux Klan. They let the black man drive the car but after about twelve miles it broke down. They left the black man in the woods tied to a tree.

The two fugitives managed to get the car started and they drove almost to Durham before they had to abandon it. At the railway yard, the pair forced a man to drive them to Winston-Salem. When they stopped to get gas, the man jumped out of the car and ran. Otto captured him again and left him tied with his belt. They knew he would soon free himself and notify the Greensboro police. The convicts continued at full speed to Winston-Salem to pick up the girl and the children. Otto planned to go to Roanoke, Virginia. Otto, his wife and children and John proceeded without trouble until they passed a car sitting by the side of the road at Schoolfield, Virginia. Otto continued on to Danville, and he and his family spent the night in the woods. The next morning, they followed an old road to Roanoke and arrived at John Starnes's home by mid-afternoon. The fugitives had been there only a few minutes when a motorcycle squad of law enforcement officers and several emergency vehicles approached the house.

The convicts ran for the railroad yards and within a few minutes they were surrounded by at least two thousand people, according to Otto. During a gunfight between the officers and the escapees, no one was hurt. Finally, Starnes was caught under a boxcar and ordered to surrender. The pair was captured and taken to jail to await the arrival of Busbee from state prison in North Carolina. This escape lost Otto the support of those who had been sympathetic to his cause and even his girlfriend turned away from him.

EIGHTH ESCAPE AND ELEVENTH ARREST

Never one to like confinement, Otto endured prison for twenty months after being captured in Roanoke. Meanwhile, his girlfriend had married a man who Otto feared would mistreat his children because he drank and had once been on the chain gang.

Otto escaped from the prison in a boxcar loaded with concrete pipes. Once outside the prison walls, he smashed a plank and jumped out onto the ground.

He remained in Raleigh long enough to board a train headed for Selma. He had a run-in with two railroad detectives but escaped, leaving his coat and hat behind. He made his way to Wadesboro, thence to Winston-Salem. He succeeded in seeing his children before going on to Brimwell, West Virginia. After a short stay, he returned to Wilkes County.

Otto was back in North Carolina when he was arrested on December 6, 1925, in Mooresville. After spending the night in the Iredell County jail, Otto was returned to prison in Raleigh.

Advice to Others

Otto wrote his autobiography in 1926 while he was serving time in the North Carolina State Prison. In it, he advised prisoners to stay and serve out their time. "Conditions may be bad and times may be dark, but it is better to endure for a while and secure freedom that will last, than it is to break away and become a miserable dodger the rest of your life, provided you manage to evade those on your trail." He wrote that it was not as easy to evade the law as it had been twenty years ago because of the International Criminal Bureau and its branches in every part of the country. Pictures of prisoners and copies of their fingerprints could now be sent to law enforcement agencies, making it harder for criminals to avoid capture. "It does not pay to run from the law," he stated. He knew from past experience that it was "better to stick around until the term is completed than escape and be brought back to start anew." Otto had learned that his mistakes "have not only brought the wages of sin upon me; they have also caused innocent women and children to suffer."

Ninth Escape and Twelfth Arrest

Otto did not take his own advice, but he escaped again from prison. On November 22, 1926, someone removed the pins from the hinges on the prison gate, and Otto was able to get out. He made his way to the Midwest. From there, he wrote letters to North Carolina newspapers offering to return to the prison in exchange for better treatment. However, North Carolina Governor A.W. McLean refused to negotiate.

Wood then attempted to rob a drugstore in Terre Haute, Indiana, and the druggist shot Wood in the chest. He would have died if the bullet had not struck the silver coins in a purse Wood had in his left vest pocket. Wood was returned to Raleigh and placed in solitary confinement on death row with armed guards posted around him twenty-four hours a day. After twenty-six months, Wood sickened and developed a hacking cough. The new governor, O. Max Gardner, visited the prison and saw that Wood's health was failing. He ordered him to be incarcerated in the regular prison compound. After that bit of kindness, Wood became a model prisoner and was put in charge of the prison canteen where he sold candy, cigarettes and the like.

TENTH AND FINAL ESCAPE

Wood gave his word of honor he would not try to escape as long as Gardner was governor. That pledge lasted only six weeks, and Otto Wood, the bandit, escaped for the fourth time from the North Carolina State Prison on July 10, 1930. Otto remained at large for six months and was declared an outlaw. A reward of $275 was offered for his capture.

AN UNTIMELY DEATH IN SALISBURY

Otto Wood met his end in the town of Salisbury, North Carolina. The papers called him the "dare-devil prison breaker." He had been outlawed and the state had put a price on his capture, either dead or alive.

The Salisbury chief of police, R.L. Rankin, had received a tip that Wood was in Salisbury, and he and the assistant chief J.W. Kestler began a search for the fugitive. It did not take them long to find him. About two o'clock in the afternoon, Wood was spotted walking with a male companion along East Innes Street in the town in front of the Yancey building, less than a block from police headquarters. Rankin stopped his car and called out to Wood to surrender, but Wood was not about to give himself up. The sheriff said, "Come here, buddy." Wood replied, "What the hell you want?" The police chief then said, "Let me see your hand." By then, Wood knew the sheriff had recognized him because the fugitive had only one hand. According to the Salisbury paper, Wood and Baker then jumped in the rear seat of the chief's car with Rankin and his assistant in the front seat. Wood ordered the policeman to "drive them out of town and keep going." Rankin hesitated for a moment, then jumped out of the car. From behind the safety of the radiator and fender, Wood exited the car and began firing. He urged his partner to do the same, but Baker did not fire.

Using his car as a shield, Rankin opened fire on Wood, and Wood fired back. When it was over, a total of eleven shots had been fired, four by Otto and seven by the officers. Wood had been fatally shot. He leg was shattered and part of his face was blown away. The officers were unharmed, although the windshield of their car was shattered. Wood was taken to the hospital in Salisbury where he expired within a few minutes. Roy Baker, Wood's companion, who identified Wood as the dead man, was put in the Rowan County jail.

The body of Otto Wood was taken to a Salisbury funeral home before it was shipped to his mother, Mrs. Ellen Wood, who lived in Coaldale, West Virginia. Wood was so well known that the people of Salisbury donated enough money to pay the funeral directors and the cost of shipping his body home. By three o'clock that afternoon, the news had spread all over town, and soon thousands of people were thronged in front of the funeral home, eager to see North Carolina's most notorious criminal.

In summarizing the criminal activities of Wood, the *Union Republican* stated that the crimes committed by the Wilkes County native had been chiefly stealing automobiles. However, seven years before his death, he had gotten in a dispute with the owner of a pawnshop and Wood had hit him in the head. Wood always swore that the blow he gave the pawnbroker "did not cause his death but that he died from other causes." Wood was given thirty years in prison for the man's death. The article concluded that Wood had escaped "four different times [from North Carolina prisons] but always came back to North Carolina and his old haunts." However, he came back one time too many and met his death from a Salisbury policeman.

Upon learning of the death of Otto Wood, W.E. Rutledge Sr., the editor of the *Yadkin Ripple*, went to Salisbury where the body could be viewed at the Wright undertaking establishment. Rutledge described what he saw: "The features of the slain desperado are much the same as in his youth, altho age and privation have made their mark on him. A bullet hole through the lower jaw showed very plainly the aim of Salisbury's chief who fired over the radiator of his car."

Poor Otto Wood! His life might have been altogether different if he had been shown the love and affection he seemed to need so much.

Immortalized in Song

The story of Otto Wood was recorded by Walter "Kid" Smith and The Carolina Buddies in February of 1931, shortly after Wood's death. "Otto Wood: The Bandit" was one of the songs on an album recorded by Doc Watson in 1999 entitled *The Best of Doc Watson*. A single was also recorded by the Elkville String Band of Wilkes County. (See the appendix for the full lyrics of the song.)

Lovers' Triangle Plus Alcohol Equals Death

East Bend Trio Are Indicted for Murder by Grand Jury

The story about the death of William Everett Dean was sandwiched on the front page of the *Yadkin Ripple* between the news of the recently drafted men from Yadkin County and the story about a Wilkes County man who was caught with six hundred gallons of "fine liquor" in his home. Dean, a thirty-five-year-old resident of East Bend, was found dead about midnight on the night of December 18, 1943, in his Ford pickup truck. The truck was discovered by Roy Smitherman and Mathew Bean, who noticed the vehicle sitting off the road because its lights were still on. The accident had occurred about halfway from Dean's home on the Shoals Road to East Bend. Roy and Mathew did not stop, but a short time later Early Vernon Sears and his brother "Snook" Sears passed by and stopped to investigate. They found the dead man in his truck with his head down on the floor and his feet in the driver's seat. At first they thought Dean was still alive and pulled him out of the truck. When they discovered he was dead, they contacted law enforcement officers.

There were several scratches and bruises on the body, and Dean's skull was fractured on the left side. This prompted the acting coroner to call for an autopsy. What at first seemed like a death due to a motor vehicle accident turned out to be a case of murder, which resulted in a search for the person or persons responsible.

Funeral services were held at the East Bend Baptist Church, after which the body was returned to Burchette & Huff Funeral Home, where the autopsy was performed. The surgeons from Bowman Gray Medical School determined that a skull fracture had caused his death. After the doctors had finished, the body was buried in the Baptist church cemetery on Wednesday.

William Everett Dean had lived in East Bend most of his life, although he was born in Thomasville, Davidson County, North Carolina, on August 30, 1908. He was employed by R.J. Reynolds Tobacco Company in the mechanical department. His father, the late W.W. Dean, had died in an accident in a furniture plant in Winston-Salem several years ago. William Dean was married to Orena Ducote, a native of Kentucky, and together they had three children. Dean was survived by his mother, Mrs. Maggie Smitherman Dean, sister Louise (both of East Bend) and a brother Sergeant Archie M. Dean, who was in the medical corps and was stationed in Cambridge, Ohio.

An inquiry into the case was called by acting coroner W.E. Rutledge, which was held on Tuesday afternoon, December 21. A jury of six men from the East Bend area attended, and they examined the autopsy report. The jury consisted of Ed M. Martin, Hovey Norman, Bob Smitherman, Dwight Martin, Brewer Hutchens and Holmes Williams. Only one witness was called at that time—Woodrow Lane. No verdict was reached, but the jury was adjourned to meet again on Thursday afternoon "for further investigation."

Coroner's Jury Orders Arrest

An inquest into the death of William Everett Dean was held at East Bend on Thursday, December 23. A number of witnesses were called to testify, including the deceased's widow and Woodrow Lane, who had lived in the Dean home for seventeen months. Several other witnesses were called in order to determine the movements of both the dead man and Lane on the night of Dean's death.

Testimony given at the inquest revealed that Dean had left home about ten o'clock. He was found shortly after midnight slumped in his truck, which had run off the road down a "small embankment." According to the surgeons who performed the autopsy, a "bad lick on the left side of his head had caused his death."

Other testimony revealed that at eleven o'clock, the truck had not been where it was found, although subsequently it was discovered at a place that was only about a five-minute drive from his home. Questions were raised as to where Dean was from ten o'clock until twelve o'clock that night. How long had he been dead when his body was discovered?

Mrs. Dean testified that her relationship with her husband was fine and denied that her husband was jealous of her relationship with Woodrow Lane. She stated that her husband had left home to sit up with Archie Johnson, a friend who was ill. She added that he was "drinking some at the time." Other evidence deemed Dean had been drinking both wine and whiskey. It was learned that Earl

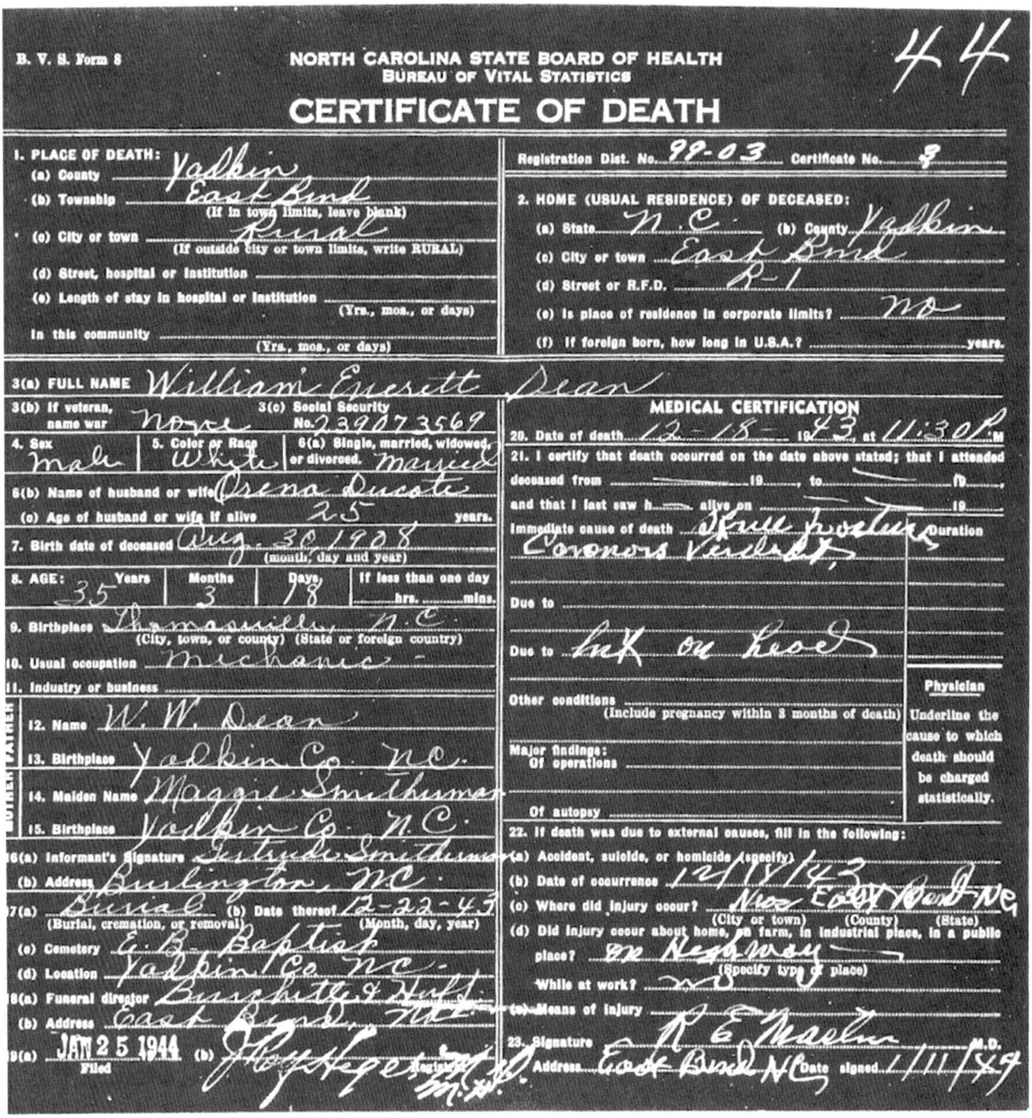

B. V. S. Form 8

NORTH CAROLINA STATE BOARD OF HEALTH
BUREAU OF VITAL STATISTICS
CERTIFICATE OF DEATH

44

1. PLACE OF DEATH: (a) County Yadkin
(b) Township East Bend (If in town limits, leave blank)
(c) City or town Rural (If outside city or town limits, write RURAL)
(d) Street, hospital or institution
(e) Length of stay in hospital or institution (Yrs., mos., or days)
In this community (Yrs., mos., or days)

Registration Dist. No. 99-03 Certificate No. 3

2. HOME (USUAL RESIDENCE) OF DECEASED: (a) State N.C. (b) County Yadkin
(c) City or town East Bend
(d) Street or R.F.D. R-1
(e) Is place of residence in corporate limits? no
(f) If foreign born, how long in U.S.A.? years.

3(a) FULL NAME William Everett Dean
3(b) If veteran, name war None 3(c) Social Security No. 239073569
4. Sex male 5. Color or Race White 6(a) Single, married, widowed, or divorced. Married
6(b) Name of husband or wife Orena Ducate
(c) Age of husband or wife if alive 25 years.
7. Birth date of deceased Aug. 30 1908 (month, day and year)
8. AGE: Years 35 Months 3 Days 18 If less than one day hrs. mins.
9. Birthplace Thomasville, N.C. (City, town, or county) (State or foreign country)
10. Usual occupation mechanic
11. Industry or business
FATHER 12. Name W. W. Dean
13. Birthplace Yadkin Co. N.C.
MOTHER 14. Maiden Name Maggie Smithurman
15. Birthplace Yadkin Co. N.C.
16(a) Informant's Signature Gertrude Smithurman
(b) Address Burlington, NC
17(a) Burial (Burial, cremation, or removal) (b) Date thereof 12-22-43 (Month, day, year)
(c) Cemetery E. B. Baptist
(d) Location Yadkin Co. N.C.
18(a) Funeral director Burchette & Huff
(b) Address East Bend, NC
19(a) JAN 25 1944 Filed (b) J. Roy Hege M.D. Registrar

MEDICAL CERTIFICATION
20. Date of death 12-18-1943, at 11:30 P.M.
21. I certify that death occurred on the date above stated; that I attended deceased from 19 , to 19 , and that I last saw h alive on 19 .
Immediate cause of death Skull fracture Duration
Coroners Verdict
Due to
Due to Lick on head
Other conditions (Include pregnancy within 3 months of death)
Major findings: Of operations
Of autopsy
Physician Underline the cause to which death should be charged statistically.
22. If death was due to external causes, fill in the following:
(a) Accident, suicide, or homicide (specify)
(b) Date of occurrence 12/18/43
(c) Where did injury occur? Near East Bend NC (City or town) (County) (State)
(d) Did injury occur about home, on farm, in industrial place, in a public place? on Highway (Specify type of place)
While at work? no
(e) Means of injury
23. Signature R. E. Martin M.D.
Address East Bend NC Date signed 1/11/44

Death certificate for William Everett Dean. *Courtesy of Yadkin County Office of Register of Deeds.*

Lineberry, his son Foster and Early Vernon "Honey" Sears had all visited the Dean home on the Saturday afternoon before the body was discovered. One of those three men, Honey Sears, was the one who got Dean out of the vehicle after it was found. Honey Sears testified that while he was in the army, he had received "about 125 letters from Mrs. Dean." He had also replied to those letters and he also wrote William Everett Dean occasionally. Why did Sears receive so many letters from Mrs. Dean? Had they been lovers before he went into the army?

A number of discrepancies were noted in the testimony of Woodrow Lane, especially regarding his whereabouts at the time Dean was killed. Lane testified that he had gone to visit Clarence Leonard, but when he approached Leonard's house, he could not see any lights on, so he returned to the Dean home. Others recalled that they had seen a light at the Leonard home from the same place that Lane said he could see no light. The jury ordered Woodrow Lane, age twenty, held without bond while the investigation into the death continued. Local officials were assisted by State Bureau of Investigation (SBI) agents Guy Scott and Lee Phillips. Dean's death certificate was not filed until January 11, 1944. The cause of death, according to the coroner's verdict, was listed as "skull fracture, due to being hit on the head."

Others active in the investigation were acting coroner Avalon E. Hall and two deputy sheriffs, Hiram Johnson and Guy Smitherman, both of East Bend. The coroner's jury resumed its hearing on Friday, January 14, 1944, and ordered that Honey Sears be arrested and held until the next term of superior court. Sears was charged with "complicity in the murder of William Everett Dean." This order was the result of two weeks of intensive investigation by Sheriff Arthur Inscore, his deputies and two SBI agents. Newspaper editor W.E. Rutledge was now the acting coroner. He replaced A.E. Hall, who became the county solicitor. Sears, age twenty-two, was a lifelong resident of East Bend, except for the five months and twenty-six days he had served in the United States Army. It is unknown why he was discharged.

Sears was put in jail but his attorney J.T. Reece obtained a writ of habeas corpus, which was presented to Judge J.A. Rousseau in Wilkesboro. However, after a routine hearing of the evidence in the case, Judge Rousseau ordered Sears "held without bond, pending action of the grand jury," which was scheduled to meet on February 7, 1944.

Testimony given by Sears had contributed to his arrest. His testimony often conflicted with statements made by both Mrs. Dean and Woodrow Lane. Sears testified that he often visited the Dean home, sometimes as many as three times a day. He said that he had been there on Saturday afternoon of the day Dean was found, but he denied allegations that he and

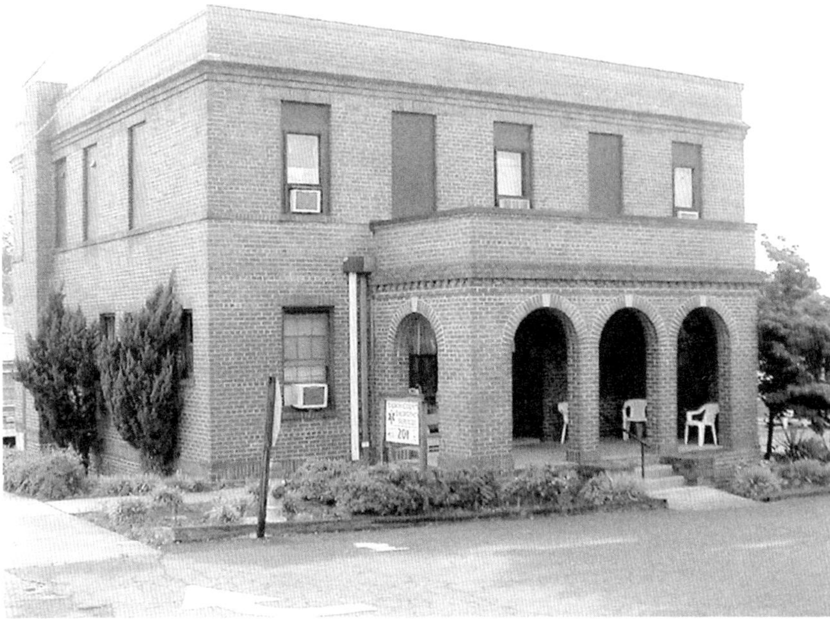

Yadkin County jail where both Lane and Sears were confined. *Photography by Frances H. Casstevens.*

Dean had had an argument and that he had been forced by Dean to leave the premises. Other witnesses testified there was much "drinking around the Dean home on the Saturday before his death." It is highly possible that this is how the murder occurred. Dean and Sears may have gotten into an argument that escalated and had fatal consequences.

SUSPICIOUS ACTIVITY UNCOVERED AND LANE TESTIFIES AGAIN

It was discovered that Mrs. Dean and Woodrow Lane had a mailbox at the Boonville post office and that they received mail there frequently. Her explanation for keeping a box there did not sound reasonable. Boonville was thirteen miles from her home. Why would she have a box at the post office there when the East Bend post office was only a few miles away? Officers also discovered that the three chopping axes Dean always kept at his woodpile had disappeared before the officer had a chance to examine Dean's home and grounds. On Tuesday, three days after Dean's death, two of the axes suddenly reappeared at the woodpile. One was still missing. Was the missing axe the murder weapon?

Woodrow Lane's mother testified at the inquest that she did not believe her son was involved in Dean's death, but she thought Woodrow knew more than he had told officers. Although being held in jail at Yadkinville, Woodrow asked to be taken to East Bend so that he could testify before the coroner's jury. His request was honored, and he was escorted to East Bend by Sheriff Inscore and Jailer W.E. Wishon. Meanwhile, Honey Sears was taken to Winston-Salem where he was fingerprinted and photographed, then returned to the Yadkin County jail.

Mrs. Dean continued to maintain that she had no idea who might have killed her husband. She also testified that she believed her husband was unfaithful. He had purchased some ladies' clothing for Christmas presents, and she knew the clothes were not for her. She concluded that Dean's death might have been the result of a "husband who was jealous of his wife and Dean." This information was unsubstantiated.

An effort to secure Lane's release on bond was denied, although his attorney W.M. Allen maintained that Lane "was being held unlawfully and without sufficient evidence." Bond for Lane was opposed by Yadkin County Solicitor Avalon E. Hall. After a hearing at the home of Judge John H. Clement in Walkertown, Lane was ordered to be returned to jail to await an inquiry before the grand jury on February 7.

Widow Arrested

Before the grand jury had a chance to meet, Mrs. Orena Ducote Dean, age twenty-four, the widow of the dead man, was arrested following the fourth session of the coroner's jury. The jury had found many discrepancies in her testimony, which also conflicted with statements made by Lane and Sears, both of whom were already being held in jail. Mrs. Dean retained Attorney Fred S. Hutchens as her legal representative. She was taken to the jail in Winston-Salem because Yadkin County had no facilities to confine women. Since the arrest of Mrs. Dean, the Yadkin County sheriff had received many "crank" phone calls from unknown persons who claimed they knew who killed William Dean.

After an investigation by Captain Burke and Lieutenant Ledwell of the Winston-Salem Police Department, it was clear that the murder did not take place in Dean's truck. But where did it take place? The woodshed with the three available lethal weapons seemed the most likely place.

Mysterious Events at the Dean Home

During the investigation, information surfaced about several mysterious events that had taken place at the Dean home: the home was almost destroyed by fire; two horses died mysteriously; and two cows, some hogs and chickens died from unknown causes. In addition, a large turkey gobbler was found dead at the home shortly after Dean's death. The cause of death of the turkey could not be determined by the officers. The investigators stated that other recently revealed information could not be revealed at this time.

The Grand Jury's Verdict

The grand jury listened to the testimony of three witnesses before handing down an indictment for the three suspects already under arrest: Mrs. Orena Dean, Woodrow Lane and Honey Sears. The three were to be held without bond until the next term of superior court. Solicitor A.E. Hall had engaged the services of Attorney A.T. Grant of Mocksville to assist in the prosecution of the case. However, by February 17, all three defendants were released on bail. Judge J.A. Rousseau announced that bond had been set at $5,000 for each of those under indictment. The amount was reduced in Mrs. Dean's case to only $2,500. Her bond was signed by Mrs. Mamie Patterson Alspaugh, formerly of East Bend. A picture of the Dean home appeared in the newspaper along with the announcement that the trio was free on bail.

Mrs. Orena Dean claimed to be Catholic, of French descent and a native of Louisiana. She stated that she and Dean were married on November 1, 1932, in Kentucky. She and Dean had been married for eleven years.

Officers Continue to Gather Evidence

Law enforcement officers continued their efforts to determine who had killed Dean. They indicated that "new evidence" had been found. Although Sheriff Inscore and SBI agent Scott were working on a new "lead," they declined to give any more information. It had been determined that the truck in which Dean was found had been pushed off the road with the lights burning, although the motor was not running. A special term of court had been called by Governor Broughton to try the case on March 27. A check of newspaper accounts for April did not mention any trial.

Superior Court Decision

The Dean murder case was the most important case scheduled to be heard at August term of Yadkin County Superior Court. However, it was doubtful that the case would be tried due to lack of evidence. Instead, it was assumed the case would be nol prossed (nolle prosequi).

This prediction proved to be correct. Judge Wilson Warlick of Newton allowed the case to be nol prossed "with leave" in case new evidence was discovered. Solicitor A.E. Hall was satisfied with that decision.

Thus ended the case of the murder of William Everett Dean. The defendants were released when a nol pros was accepted. The Dean case could always be reopened if sufficient evidence was found to determine who had killed the victim. No new evidence was found. Since there is no statute of limitation in a murder case, the case remains open today.

Lingering Questions

Why did Mrs. Dean and Woodrow Lane keep another post office box? With whom were they corresponding? Were they taking orders for moonshine whiskey or selling rationed goods on the black market. Why was Honey Sears a frequent visitor to the Dean home? He stated that he visited the home when Mr. Dean was away as much as three times a day. Surely something more than sex was going on inside the house.

Why were the Deans' animals dying? Were they poisoned or did they die from neglect? Was their death due to natural causes or did someone have a grudge against the Deans (either William or his wife, or both)?

Where had Dean actually been killed? Was the murder weapon the missing axe? Did the three suspects escape punishment due to lack of evidence, or was the crime committed by someone else, as indicated by Mrs. Dean?

This case is only one of many unsolved murder mysteries. Probably, the truth will never be known. By now, the murderer is probably dead and unavailable for punishment on this Earth.

Appendix: Crime Poems and Songs

Untitled folk version of Tom Dula story

Originally in Manley Wade Wellman's *Dead and Gone.*

Oh, bow your head, Tom Dula,
Oh, bow your head and cry;
You've killed poor Laura Foster
And you know you're bound to die.

I take my banjo this evening,
I pick it on my knee;
This time tomorrow evening
'Twill be no use to me.

I had my trial at Wilkeboro,
Oh, what do you reckon they done?
They bound me over to Statesville
And there's where I'll be hung.

Oh, pappy, oh, pappy,
What shall I do?
I have lost all my money
And killed poor Laura, too.

Oh, mammy, oh, mammy,
Bow your head and cry.
I've killed poor Laura Foster
And I know I'm bound to die.

Oh, what my mammy told me
Is about to come to pass;
That drinking and the women
Would be my ruin at last.

TOM DOOLEY

Originally a traditional ballad, revised by Frank Proffit, recorded by Frank Warner and later the Kingston Trio in 1958.

Chorus: Hang down your head, Tom Dooley,
Hang down your head and cry;
Hang down your head, Tom Dooley,
Poor boy, you're bound to die.

I met her on the mountain,
There I took her life;
Met her on the mountain,
Stabbed her with my knife.

Repeat Chorus

This time tomorrow,
Reckon where I'll be;
Hadn't a-been for Grayson,
I'd a-been in Tennessee.

Repeat Chorus

This time tomorrow,
Reckon where I'll be;
Down in some lonesome valley,
Hangin' from a white oak tree.

Repeat Chorus

THE MURDER OF WILL KELLY

By Frances H. Casstevens

I composed a poem about the tragedy on December 7, 1975, before I had begun to research the events that occurred at the now famous Dalton-Hunt house.

Will Kelly was the young man's name,
His father was a farmer.
Will had no money to his name,
But he was a charmer.

He charmed Miss Daisy and he won
Her love and adoration.
He'd marry her tonight he said,
Without much preparation.

He courted her in secrecy,
Her love she gladly gave.
She never thought t'would be her love
That sent him to his grave.

Miss Daisy said, "Please, Mama dear,
You'd better let me marry,
So I can give a decent name
To this child I carry."

"I'll never let you marry Will.
I'll see him in his grave
Before he weds a girl of mine,"
Was the answer that she gave.

Will wrote a letter to his love.
He waited for an answer,
And as he waited patiently,
A bullet was his answer.

T'was a snowy winter night,
The year was 1902.
A shot flashed through pale moonlight—
Or maybe there were two.

Miss Daisy, locked up in her room,
Could see the gory sight.
Her lover dying slowly there
In the barn that night.

They would not let her go to him,
She tried with all her might,
But from her window she did watch
Her lover through the night.

Her Uncle Will, was said by some,
Had done this bloody deed,
For from the country he did flee
Upon his big white steed.

The child she bore in early spring,
The ruin of them all,
Marked by the sight of blood, t'was said,
It stained his very soul.

POOR ELLEN SMITH

Traditional Tom Sauber version, from article by Bob Waltz, *Inside Bluegrass,* August 2002.

[Sung to the tune of *How Firm a Foundation*]

Poor Ellen Smith, and it's how she was found,
Shot through the heart, lying cold on the ground.
Oh, I brushed back my tears when the people all said
That Peter DeGraff had shot Ellen Smith dead.

While I would have loved her and made her my wife,
Lord, I loved her too dearly to take her sweet life.
They grabbed their Winchesters, they hunted me down,
But I was away in old Mount Airy town.

They carried me to Winston, my trial to stand
To live or to die as the law may command.
McArthur will harm me, he will if he can;
God knows if they hang me, I'll die an innocent man.

THE LAWSON FAMILY IN RHYME

By Edith Willard, printed in *The Yadkin Ripple*, January 23, 1929.

In the little county of Walnut Cove
Not very far away,
There happened an awful tragedy
On a snowy Christmas day.

Charles Lawson wiped out every member
Of his family except one son,
Then it seemed as though he realized
The awful deed that he had done.

Mrs. Lawson, Marie and Raymond
Were lying on the floor,
And James William who tried to escape
Was shot outside the door.

Little Mary Lou the baby
Was only five months old,
Was found within the cradle
So lifeless and so cold.

Carrie and Maybelle were shot down
As rabbits in the snow,
They were headed for their uncle's
As their little footprints show.

It was near the tobacco barn
The little girls were slain,
They were taken into the barn
And there their bodies were lain.

Upon the cold and bare earth
With their hands folded across their breast,
With rocks as their pillows
More peacefully to rest.

The little nice blue hat
Which Carrie often wore,
Was crumpled and bloodstained
Which she would wear no more.

The father returning to the house
And saw that all were dead
He took the snow-white pillows
And placed them under their heads.

Young Arthur, their son, went to Germantown
To buy some shells for a gun,
But before he had returned
He heard of the deed that was done.

They were all devoted to each other
Arthur loved them every one,
Bul he is left here alone
And their work on earth is done.

The neighbors were very troubled
For they would see their face no more,
All Stokes County was stirred
As it never was stirred before.

A spot in the woods not far away
Where Lawson's body was found,
With a shot gun wound through his heart
Lying cold on the ground.

They were buried in white caskets
Which were white as the snow
And a kind man's word of comfort
Says, "God Only Knows."

They were buried in Browder's Graveyard
Upon a little nole,
They were placed side by side
In the ground so dark and cold.

They have gone beyond our presence
Beneath the silent clay,
And God knows the secret
Which will be revealed some day.

OTTO WOOD: THE BANDIT

Recorded by Walter "Kid" Smith and The Carolina Buddies in February of 1931.

Step up buddies and listen to my song
I'll sing it to you right, but you may sing it wrong,
All about a man named Otto Wood,
I can't tell you all, but I wish I could.

He walked in a pawnshop a rainy day,
And with the clerk he had a quarrel, they say.
Pulled out his pistol and he struck him a blow,
And this is the way the story goes.

They spread the news as fast as they could,
The sheriff served a warrant on Otto Wood.
The jury said murder in the second degree,
And the judge passed the sentence to the penitentiary.

They put him in the pen, but it done no good,
It wouldn't hold the man they called Otto Wood.
It wasn't very long till he slipped outside,
Drawed a gun on the guard, said, "Take me for a ride."

Second time they caught him was away out west,
In the holdup game, he got shot through the breast.
They brought him back and when he got well,
They locked him down in a dungeon cell.

He was a man they could not run,
He always carried a .44 gun.
He loved the women and hated the law,
And he just wouldn't take nobody's jaw.

He rambled out west and he rambled all around,
He met the sheriff in a Southern town.
And the sheriff says, "Otto, step this way,
'Cause I've been expecting you every day."

He pulled out his gun and then he said,
"If you make a crooked move, you both fall dead.
Crank up your car and take me out of town,"
And a few minutes later, he was graveyard bound.

Otto, why didn't you run?
Otto's done dead and gone.
Otto Wood, why didn't you run
When the sheriff pulled out his .44 gun?

Bibliography

Unpublished Manuscripts and Government Records

1850 Federal Census, Wilkes County, North Carolina.

1860 Federal Census, Caldwell County, North Carolina.

1860 Federal Census, Yadkin County, North Carolina.

DeGraff, Peter, file. North Carolina Room, Forsyth County Public Library, Winston-Salem, NC.

Pension Application Papers of Sarah C. Dobbins, Widow, National Archives, Washington, D.C.

Richmond M. Pearson Collection, Duke University, Durham, NC.

Samuel Speer Family Bible, Frances H. Casstevens collection.

State v. Dula, North Carolina Reports, Archive 1778–1968, records of Supreme Court, 1867, 1868.

Surry County, North Carolina, Deeds and Marriage Records.

Yadkin County, North Carolina, Deeds, Death Certificates and Court Records.

Books

Absher, W.O., ed. *The Heritage of Wilkes County, North Carolina.* Winston-Salem, NC: Hunter Publishing, 1982.

Alexander, Nancy. *Tom Dooley*. Lenoir, NC: News-Topic, 1959.

Belden, Henry M., and Arthur Palmer Hudson, eds. *The Frank C. Brown Collection of North Carolina Folklore.* Vol. 2. Durham, NC: Duke University Press, 1952.

Bradshaw, Jon. *Dreams That Money Can Buy: The Tragic Life of Libby Holman.* New York: William Morrow & Co., 1985.

Brumfield, Lewis S. *Historical Architecture of Yadkin County, North Carolina.* Winston-Salem, NC: Winston Publishing, 1985.

———. "Thomas Lanier Clingman and the Shallow Ford Families." Yadkinville, NC: Privately published, 1989.

Hayes, John J. *The Land of Wilkes.* Charlotte, NC: Heritage Printers, 1962.

Hoots, Carl C., compl. *Cemeteries of Yadkin County, North Carolina.* Spartanburg, SC: The Reprint Co., 1985.

Jones, M. Bruce, and Trudy J. Smith. *White Christmas, Bloody Christmas.* Trinity, NC: UpWords Publications, 1990.

Lefler, Hugh T., and Albert Ray Newsome. *North Carolina: The History of a Southern State.* Chapel Hill: University of North Carolina Press, 1973.

Lomax, Alan, ed. *Folk Song: U. S.A.* New York: Duell, Sloan and Pearce, 1947.

Machlin, Milt. *Libby.* New York: Tower Productions, 1980.

Manarin, Louis H., and Weymouth T. Jordan, comps. *North Carolina Troops, 1861–1865: A Roster.* 15 vols. Raleigh: North Carolina Department of Archives and History, 1966–1998.

McCracken, Anne Whitaker, comp. *1880 Federal Census of Yadkin County, North Carolina.* Marietta, GA: Chestnut Ridge Research, 1991.

Perry, Hamilton Darby. *Libby Holman: Body and Soul.* Boston, MA: Little, Brown & Co., 1983.

Renegar, Michael. *Roadside Revenants and Other North Carolina Legends.* Fairview, NC: Bright Mountain Books, Inc., 2005.

Reynolds, Karen Wheeling. *Tom Dooley: A Wilkes County Legend.* Wilkesboro, NC: Thursday Printing, Inc., 2002.

Rutledge, William E., ed. "An Illustrated History of Yadkin County, 1850–1965." 1st ed. Yadkinville, NC: Privately published, 1965.

Tursi, Frank V. *Winston-Salem: A History.* Winston-Salem, NC: John F. Blair, 1994.

West, John Foster. *The Ballad of Tom Dula: The Documented Story Behind the Murder of Laura Foster and the Trials and Execution of Tom Dula.* Boone, NC: Parkway Publishers, 2002.

———. *Lift Up Your Head, Tom Dooley.* Asheboro, NC: Down Home Press, 1993.

Wood, Otto. *A True History of My Life, Ranging from Four Years Old up till the Present.* Raleigh, NC: Commercial Printing Co., 1926.

NEWSPAPER ARTICLES

"Aftermath of the Lawson Tragedy." *Union Republican*, January 16, 1930.

"All Defendants Free on Bail." *Yadkin Ripple*, February 17, 1944.

"Coroner's Hearing in Dean's Death to Resume Friday." *Yadkin Ripple*, January 13, 1944.

"Coroner says Reynolds Killed Self; Sheriff's Investigation of Death Continues." *Winston-Salem Journal*, July 7, 1932.

"Criminal Court Ends Tuesday." *Yadkin Ripple*, August 24, 1944.

"'Dead' Man Turns up Here to End One Phase of Two Year Yadkin County Mystery." *Yadkin Ripple*, May 8, 1941.

"The Death Penalty." *New York Herald*, May 2, 1868.

"The Death Penalty." *Salisbury* [NC] *Watchman and Old North State*, May 8, 1868.

"East Bend Man is Found Dead on Sat. Night." *Yadkin Ripple*, December 23, 1943.

"East Bend Trio Are Indicted for Murder by Grand Jury Here." *Yadkin Ripple*, February 10,1944.

East, Bill. "Execution Order is Found." *Winston-Salem Journal*, 1975.

———. "Man Recalls Hanging." *Winston-Salem Journal and Sentinel*, April 20, 1975.

"Editor Rutledge Sees Wood's Body." *Yadkin Ripple*, January 1, 1931.

"Eight Members of One Family Sleep in Huge Grave in Stokes County." *Union Republican*, January 2, 1930.

"Fence Around Lawson House." *Yadkin Ripple*, January 23, 1930.

Gaston, Janice. "Bloody Christmas: The horror of that cold day in '29 can still send chills down the spine." *Winston-Salem Journal*, December 22, 1991.

"He Killed Ellen. DeGraff Makes a Confession on Scaffold." *Winston-Salem Sentinel*, February 8, 1894.

Hicks, Glenna. "Lawson Recalls 1929 Christmas Tragedy." *Danbury Reporter*, August 18, 1977.

"'Honey' Sears is Held by Coroners Jury: Judge Rousseau Denies Bond." *Yadkin Ripple*, January 20, 1944.

"Inquest May Be Held Later." *Winston-Salem Journal*, July 7, 1932.

"Judge Denies Lane Freedom." *Yadkin Ripple*, January 27, 1944.

"Judge Warlick to Hold Court Here Monday." *Yadkin Ripple*, August 17, 1944.

Julia Dalton and Henry Gorman, marriage announcement in *Western Carolinian*, September 6, 1839.

Kaufman, Tamera. "Christmas Murder Story is Best Seller: Tale of Lawson Family Tragedy Intrigued Author for Years." *Weekly Independent*, February 7, 1991.

"Kramer Says Intruder May Have Entered." *Winston-Salem Journal*, July 14, 1932.

"Lane is Held in Dean Death." *The Yadkin Ripple*, December 30, 1943.

Minick, Ruth. "Peter DeGraff was Hanged for Murder." *Times Weekly*, April 5, 1984.

Moorehouse, Ward. "Smith Reynolds' Widow Breaks Silence for First Time since July 6." *New York Sun*, September 24, 1932.

"Mrs. Dean is Jailed After Fourth Hearing." *Yadkin Ripple*, February 3, 1944.

"Mystery of Dead Man Found Near Here in Woods Still Unsolved." *Yadkin Ripple*, August 10, 1939.

"Negro is Held for Murder of Children." *Yadkin Ripple*, January 30, 1947.

"New Evidence in Dean Case, Says Sheriff Inscore." *Yadkin Ripple*, February 24, 1944.

"Officers Hold Albert Walker for Testimony." *Winston-Salem Journal*, July 9, 1932.

"Otto Wood Slain by Salisbury Officer." *The Union Republican*, January 8, 1931.

"Peter DeGraff is Still at Liberty." *Salem People's Press*, August 4, 1892.

"Poindexter Buys Old Dr. Hunt Home at Huntsville." *The Yadkin Ripple*, April 22, 1943.

"Rites Held for Bruce Davis December 24." *Yadkin Ripple*, January 3, 1974.

Rutledge, Ed. "Man from Center Watched Hanging of Peter Degraff." 1960, reprinted in *Yadkin Ripple*, October 26, 2000.

———. "Tragedy Strikes Proud Hunt Family: Murder of Will Kelly is Still Unsolved." *Yadkin Ripple*, September 28, 1950.

"Scene of Stokes County's Worst Tragedy." *Winston-Salem Journal*, December 28, 1929.

"Scott Receives Crank Letters." *Winston-Salem Journal*, July 18, 1932.

"Smith Reynolds Shot in Head; Condition Serious." *Winston-Salem Journal*, July 6, 1932.

Sparks, Jim. "1868 Hanging: Lift of your head, Tom Dula, you might get a pardon." *Winston-Salem Journal*, June 27, 2001.

"Thinks All Evidence in Case Points to Suicide." *Winston-Salem Journal*, July 8, 1932.

"Tragedy." *Stanley News and Press*, reprinted in *Yadkin Ripple*, January 16, 1930.

Tursi, Frank. "The Tragic Story of Jack Hunt." *The Clemons* [NC] *Courier*, February 14, 1974.

"Widow Leaves, Departs on Afternoon Train for Cincinnati." *Winston-Salem Journal*, July 18, 1932.

"Widow May be Out of Legacy." *Winston-Salem Journal*, July 7, 1932.

"Williams Faces Murder Charge After Tuesday Morning Shooting." *Yadkin Ripple*, August 31, 1961.

Willis, Alan. "'Hear My Dying Words,' Sensational Murder Case Ended 85 Years Ago." *Winston-Salem Sentinel*, February 8, 1979.

"Yadkin's Mystery Man of 1939 is Still Mystery Man in 1940." *Yadkin Ripple*, August 1, 1940.

"Yadkin's New Mystery is Yet Unsolved: Might be McDouglall; Ripple Makes Important Find." *Yadkin Ripple*, August 3, 1939.

"Z. Smith Reynolds Portrait Unveiled." *Winston-Salem Journal*, May 9, 1964.

Periodicals

The Carolina Farmer, August 1960.

Casstevens, Frances H. "Through Some Very Lonely Looking Wood: The Story of a Yadkin County Family's Journey Through Tennessee." *The North Carolina Genealogical Society Journal* 16, no. 2 (May 1990): 91–94.

Craaybeek, Wanda. "Our Speer Connection." *Our Heritage and History*, no. 3 (May 1989).

Selected Internet Sources

Barnett, Rich. "The DuPont, The Torch Singer, and The Tobacco Heir." http://www.camprehoboth.com/issue08_26_05/camp_stories.htm

"A Brief History of the Christopher Reynolds Foundation." http://www.creynolds.org/history.htm

Moran, Faye Jarvis. "Who Was Anny Foster." http://www.fmoran.com/wilkes/anny.html

Reynolda House Museum of American Art. http://www.reynoldahouse.org/

"Tom Dula." *Wilkes Chamber of Commerce*. http:// www.wilkesnc.org/history/tomdula/

Turner, Walter R. "Development of Streetcar Systems in North Carolina." *Charlotte-Mecklenburg Historic Landmarks Commission*. http://www.cmhpf.org/development%20of%20streetcar%20systems.htm

Books by Frances H. Casstevens

Local History

Ghosts and their Haunts: The Legends and Lore of the Yadkin River Valley, Boone, NC: Parkway Publishing Co., 2005 (distributed by John F. Blair & Co.).

Heritage of Yadkin County, North Carolina, Vol. I. Winston-Salem, NC: Hunter Publishing Co., 1981.

Yadkin County, North Carolina: The First One Hundred Years. Dover, NH: Arcadia Publishing Co., 1996.

Civil War Books (McFarland & Co., Jefferson, NC)

The Civil War and Yadkin County, North Carolina, 1997.

Clingman's Brigade in the Confederacy, 1862–1865, 2002.

Edward A. Wild and the African Brigade in the Civil War, 2003.

George Washington Alexander and Castle Thunder: A Prison and its Commandant, 2004.

"Out of the Mouth of Hell": Civil War Prisons and Escapes, 2005.

Tales from the North and South: Twenty-four Remarkable People and Events of the Civil War, in press.